符号中国 SIGNS OF CHINA

文房清供

STATIONERY AND BIBELOT IN ANCIENT STUDIES

"符号中国"编写组 ◎ 编著

中央民族大学出版社
China Minzu University Press

图书在版编目(CIP)数据

文房清供：汉文、英文 / "符号中国"编写组编著. —北京：
中央民族大学出版社, 2024.8
（符号中国）
ISBN 978-7-5660-2357-5

Ⅰ.①文… Ⅱ.①符… Ⅲ.①文化用品—介绍—中国—汉、英 Ⅳ.①K875.4

中国国家版本馆CIP数据核字（2024）第016698号

符号中国： 文房清供 STATIONERY AND BIBELOT IN ANCIENT STUDIES

编 著	"符号中国"编写组
策划编辑	沙 平
责任编辑	陈 琳
英文指导	李瑞清
英文编辑	邱 械
美术编辑	曹 娜 郑亚超 洪 涛
出版发行	中央民族大学出版社
	北京市海淀区中关村南大街27号　　邮编：100081
	电话：（010）68472815（发行部）　传真：（010）68933757（发行部）
	（010）68932218（总编室）　　　　（010）68932447（办公室）
经 销 者	全国各地新华书店
印 刷 厂	北京兴星伟业印刷有限公司
开 本	787 mm×1092 mm 1/16　印张：10.5
字 数	145千字
版 次	2024年8月第1版　2024年8月第1次印刷
书 号	ISBN 978-7-5660-2357-5
定 价	58.00元

版权所有 侵权必究

"符号中国"丛书编委会

唐兰东　巴哈提　杨国华　孟靖朝　赵秀琴

本册编写者

茅翊

前言 Preface

中国是一个具有悠久历史的文明古国，中国人民创造出了无数的文化艺术瑰宝，形成了独具特色的中华文化。其中就包括中国特有的书法和国画艺术，而书法和国画，历来都是用中国传统的书写工具笔、墨、纸、砚及其他文房用具来完成的。

As a country with an ancient civilization, Chinese people created numerous cultural and artistic treasures that formed their distinctive national culture, which include the unique calligraphy and Chinese painting that for all the times, are accomplished by traditional Chinese writing appliances: writing brush, ink stick, paper, inkstone and other study stationery.

Aside from writing brush, ink stick, paper and inkstone, there also include several auxiliary stationery, like water-infusing tools, writing brush container, writing brush

1

除了笔、墨、纸、砚，中国传统的文房用具还包括一些辅助用具，如注水器具、笔筒、笔架、墨床、砚山、镇纸等，这些用具被泛称为"文房清供"。它们又因为有着精美的工艺造型和观赏性而被称为"文玩"。文房清供材质丰富，器型繁多，用途广泛，所用材料包括玉、石、金属、漆、陶瓷、玻璃、珐琅，以及竹、木、牙、匏等品类；制作工艺繁复，涵盖了铸造、雕刻、琢制等加工工艺。

文房清供同笔、墨、纸、砚一起，组成了一个绮丽多姿的艺术品世界，显示出了中华文化的魅力。

rack, ink rest, ink rockwork, paperweight, etc., which are called stationery and bibelot in ancient studies. Additionally, due to their delicate craft and modeling as well as the ornamental value, they are known as cultural antique as well. They are produced from various materials and with plentiful styles and broad application scope. Many materials including jade, stone, metal, lacquer, porcelain, glass, enamel, as well as bamboo, wood, ivory, calabash, etc., are applied in the production. The craftsmanship is also complicated which involves many processing techniques like foundry, sculpture and carving, etc.

Stationery and bibelot in ancient studies, along with writing brush, ink stick, paper and inkstone, constitute a gorgeous world of artwork and exhibit the charm of Chinese culture.

目 录 Contents

文房清供的历史
History of Stationery and Bibelot in Ancient Studies 001

文房与文房用具
Studies and Study Appliances 002

文房清供的历史
History of Stationery and
Bibelot in Ancient Studies 014

文房清供的品类
Categorization of Stationery and Bibelot in Ancient Studies 031

与笔相关的文房用具
Study Appliances Associated
with Writing Brush.. 032

与墨相关的文房用具
Study Appliances
Associated with Ink Stick 048

与纸相关的文房用具
Study Appliances Associated
with Paper 051

与砚相关的文房用具
Study Appliances
Associated with Inkstone 062

其他文房用具
Other Study Appliances..................................... 076

文房清供的材质及制作工艺
Materials and Craftsmanship of Stationery
and Bibelot in Ancient Studies..........089

金属
Metal 090

陶瓷
Ceramics 094

玉
Jade 109

漆
Lacquer 114

石
Stone 118

竹
Bamboo 126

木
Wood 132

象牙
Ivory 136

匏
Gourd 141

附录：书房陈设品
Appendix: Antiques in Studies 143

文房清供的历史
History of Stationery and Bibelot in Ancient Studies

中国文房清供的历史十分悠久,并且与社会、经济和文化一同发展,在实践中被不断完善,最终成为内涵丰富,具有实用和观赏价值的艺术品。

The history of the stationery and bibelot in ancient studies of China is fairly long. They developed along with the social progress and the prosperity of economy and culture, improved consecutively in practices, and finally became a kind of artwork with rich connotations and possessing both functional and ornamental values.

> 文房与文房用具

在中国古代，学识渊博、崇尚风雅的人被称为"文人"，"文房"就是文人的书房。不过，最早

> Studies and Study Appliances

In ancient China, men with profound knowledge and elegant taste were called literati (*Wenren*, *Wen* for literacy, *Ren* for person); and study (*Wenfang*,

• 传统文房摆设
Traditional Stationery and Furniture in the Study

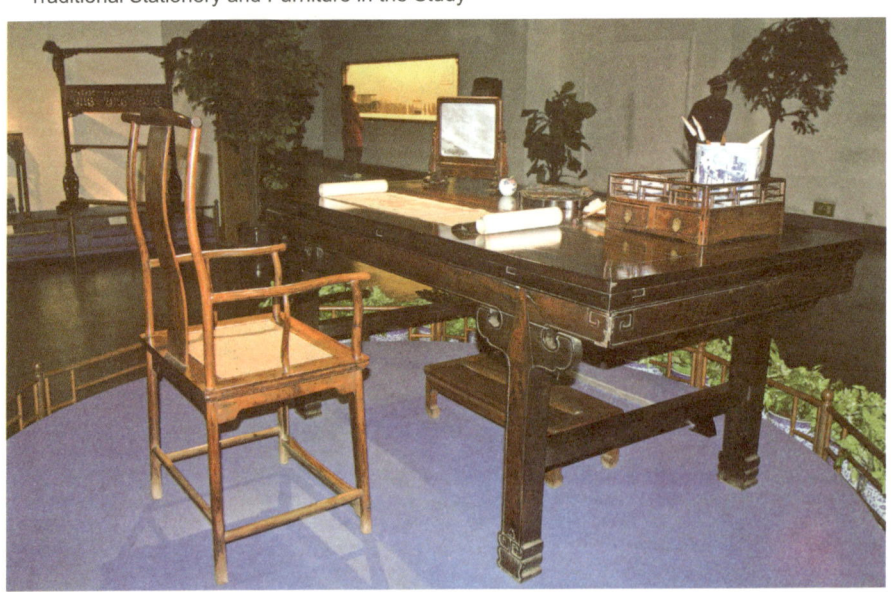

• 文房用具架（清·乾隆）
Shelves for Study Appliances (Qianlong Period, Qing Dynasty, 1736-1795)

的文房并不是文人的书房。在南北朝时期，《梁书·江革传》《南史·卷六十八·列传第五十八》中都提及过"文房"一词，指国家掌管文书的地方。到了唐代，"文房"一词除了上述之意，开始专指文人的书房。南唐后主李煜喜爱文学，收藏了很多书画作品。他在所藏的书画上均押以"建业文房之印"，这时的文房已成为鉴赏书画，收藏书籍、绘画和书法的地方。

中国的书法和国画是世界文化史上独具风格的艺术形式，都是用独具特色的传统书写工具——笔、墨、纸、砚来完成的。自古以来，笔、墨、纸、砚被称为"文房四宝"。毛笔是中国古代书写文字

Fang for room) indicated the study of literati. However, as mentioned in historical books like the *Book of Liang: Biography of Jiang Ge*, and the *History of Southern Dynasties: Volume 68, the 58th Biographies,* the term *Wenfang* in initial age didn't refer to the study; it specifically indicated the administration that managed the official document. By the Tang Dynasty (618-907), besides the above meaning, it started to refer to the study of literati. Li Yu, the last ruler of the Southern Tang Kingdom (937-975), was fond of literature and had a large collection of works of calligraphy and Chinese painting, on which he stamped with the *Seal of Jianye Wenfang*. At that time, *Wenfang* became the place where people appreciated and stored works of calligraphy and paintings, as well as books and records.

Chinese calligraphy and painting are arts of distinctive feature in the world's artistic history. Both of them are accomplished by the exclusive writing appliances: writing brush, ink stick, paper and inkstone, which have been called the Scholar's Four Jewels ever since ancient times. The writing brush is a basic tool for writing and painting in ancient China, which is composed of brush head,

和绘画的基本工具。毛笔由笔头、笔管和笔帽组成。笔头是用来蘸墨写字和绘画的部分，由动物的毛制成。笔管是手握笔的部分，一端装有笔头，是毛笔装饰性最强的部分，多以竹、木、牙、陶瓷、珐琅等各种材质制成。笔帽即笔套，用来保护笔头不受损坏。

墨是中国书法和绘画的主要工具，有历久不褪色的特点。正是在墨的作用下，中国的书法和绘画作品才形成了独特的艺术风格。墨分黑色墨、彩色墨和药用墨，早期的

- 乾隆御咏名花诗十色墨（清）
Ink Sticks of Ten Colors with *Themes of Ten Odes of Famous Flowers* Written by Emperor Qianlong (Qing Dynasty, 1616-1911)

笔管 Brush Penholder　　笔头 Brush Head　　笔帽 Brush Cap

- 竹管笔（宋）
Writing Brush with a Bamboo Penholder (Song Dynasty, 960-1279)

penholder and cap. The brush head is the part used to dip ink for writing and drawing, which is made from the hair of animals. The penholder is the part for gripping and in which the brush head is fitted. The penholder often is decorated with complicated garnishes, and is mostly made of bamboo, wood, ivory, porcelain, enamel, etc. The cap, also the brush cap, is used to protect the brush head from damage.

The ink stick is a major tool for Chinese calligraphy and painting, with the feature of fadelessness for thousands of years. Due to the ink stick, Chinese calligraphy and painting are able to possess distinct artistic style. It includes black, colorized and officinal ones. Ink sticks of the early stage were made from natural graphite. Then later, it

大清宣统御制宣纸
Imperial Rice Paper in the Xuantong Period of the Qing Dynasty

墨由天然石墨制作，后来出现了人工制成的松烟墨、油烟墨等。

造纸术是中国对人类文明做出的重大贡献之一，与火药、指南针、印刷术并称为中国古代科学技术的四大发明。纸的发明在人们的生活中起到了重要作用，使中国文化得以弘扬、传播。造纸术的西传还推动了世界文化的发展。在传统的文房用纸中，宣纸著称于世。宣纸至迟在唐代便开始生产，从唐代

appeared the synthetic pine-soot ink and lampblack ink, etc.

Invented by Chinese people, papermaking technology is one of the greatest contributions to human civilization, along with gunpowder, compass and printing technology, which is considered as the Four Great Inventions of ancient Chinese science and technology. The invention of paper played an important role in people's daily life. It made Chinese culture spread abroad

《天工开物》中记载的竹纸制法

《天工开物》是中国古代一部综合性的科学技术著作，初刊于明代崇祯十年（1637年），作者是明代的科学家宋应星。全书叙述了各种农作物和工业原料的种类、产地、生产技术、工艺装备等，被称为"中国17世纪的工艺百科全书"。书中详细记载了用竹子造纸的工艺过程，共有5个步骤：

1.斩竹漂塘：斩下嫩竹放入池中浸泡百日以上。

2.煮楻足火：将泡好的竹子放入桶内，与石灰一道蒸煮八日八夜。

3.荡料入帘：将打烂的竹料倒入水槽内，并以竹帘在水中荡料，使竹料成为薄层，附于竹帘上面。

4.覆帘压纸：将竹帘翻过去，使湿竹料薄层落于板上，即成一张纸。如此重复，一张张湿纸叠积至上千张，然后在纸上加木板重压，挤去水分。

5.透火焙干：将湿纸逐张揭开，贴在由土砖砌成的夹巷墙上，在巷中生火，将湿纸焙干。

Bamboo Papermaking Method Documented in
Exploitation of the Works of Nature

Exploitation of the Works of Nature is a miscellaneous work on ancient Chinese science and technology written by Song Yingxing in the tenth year of the Chongzhen Period (1637) of the Ming Dynasty (1368-1644). The book refers to various species of crops and industrial raw materials and records their place of origin, production technique and processing equipment, hence known as the Technical Encyclopedia of the 17th Century China. Particularly it documents in detail the process of bamboo papermaking, five steps in total as follows:

1.Cut and Soak: Cut down the tender bamboo and soak it in the pool for a hundred days or more.

2.Stew with Lime: Put the well-soaked bamboo into a barrel. Stew it with lime for eight days and eight nights.

3.Sweep the Mash: Pour the bamboo mash into the tank, sweep it over with a bamboo screen, and then a thin layer of bamboo material will attach to the screen.

4.Turn and Press: Turn over the screen so that the wet paper can fall onto a board. Then repeat the process over and again, till thousands of pieces accumulate into a thick pile. Squeeze the water out by a heavy wood.

5.Bake and Dry: Take off the wet paper piece by piece. Attach them to the brick walls on both sides of the lane. Make a fire to dry the wet paper.

《天工开物》插图——斩竹漂塘

Illustration in *Exploitation of the Works of Nature*: Cut and Soak

- 《天工开物》插图——煮楻足火
Illustration in *Exploitation of the Works of Nature*: Stew with Lime

- 《天工开物》插图——荡料入帘
Illustration in *Exploitation of the Works of Nature*: Sweep the Mash

- 《天工开物》插图——覆帘压纸
Illustration in *Exploitation of the Works of Nature*: Turn and Press

- 《天工开物》插图——透火焙干
Illustration in *Exploitation of the Works of Nature*: Bake and Dry

开始便是书画的主流用纸，受到历代文人、书画家的青睐。

砚是用于磨墨、盛墨和蘸墨的书写用具。砚历史悠久，种类很多，有瓦砚、陶砚、砖砚、瓷砚、石砚、玉砚、漆砂砚、铜砚、铁砚

• 褐釉兽座箕形瓷砚（唐）
Dustpan-shaped and Brown-glazed Porcelain Inkstone with Animal-shaped Stand (Tang Dynasty, 618-907)

• 石砚（唐）
Inkstone (Tang Dynasty, 618-907)

and also promoted the development of the world culture. Among the traditional papers used in studies, the rice paper is well-known to the world, which has started to be produced no later than the Tang Dynasty. Since then, rice paper has become the main paper used for Chinese calligraphy and painting and was favored by literati and masters of successive dynasties.

The inkstone is a type of writing tool used for ink-grind, ink-filling, ink-dip and adjustment of brush hair. With a fairly long history, it has various kinds, including tile inkstone, ceramic inkstone, brick inkstone, porcelain inkstone, jade inkstone, lacquer-emery inkstone (a wooden in slab coated with the mixture of emery and lacquer), copper inkstone, iron inkstone, etc. The modeling of the inkstone is ingenious and original. Aside from the multi-foot, round, square, dustpan-shaped and hand-held ones, there also exists zither-shaped, drum-shaped, bamboo joint-shaped, bamboo shoot-shaped, leechee-shaped, lotus leaf-shaped, banana leaf-shaped, cat-shaped and bell-shaped inkstones. Patterns carved on the inkstone are varied in a wide range of themes which include

等。砚的造型奇巧而独特，除了多足砚、圆形砚、方形砚、箕形砚、抄手砚，还有琴式、鼓式、竹节形、竹笋形、荔枝形、荷叶形、蕉叶形、猫形、钟形砚等。砚的题材内容也非常广泛，有云龙日月、飞禽和走兽、花鸟和鱼虫、山川景物、历史典故、金石书画等。砚的雕刻技法多样，包括圆雕、深雕、镂空雕、浮雕、阴刻等。

除了笔、墨、纸、砚，文房中还常见一些辅助的用具，例如盛装研墨用清水的器具、搁置蘸墨毛笔的器具、压镇宣纸的器具，等等。这些辅助用具可谓琳琅满目、包罗万象、用途广泛，如水注、水丞、墨盒、墨床、镇纸、压尺、诗筒、笔筒、笔插、笔架、笔挂、笔洗、笔掭、臂搁、裁纸刀、糊斗、印章、印盒、帖架、文具箱等。其材质也丰富多彩，种类繁多，有金属、竹、木、陶瓷、玉、石、玻璃、珐琅、漆等。这些具有实用和观赏价值的文房陈设品，被泛称为"文房清供"，受到历代文人的喜爱和帝王的珍视。

• 十二兽足台砚
Platform Inkstone with Twelve Animal-shaped Feet

• "长乐未央"瓦当砚（清）
Eaves Tile Inkstone Made from the Tile of Changle Palace (Qing Dynasty, 1616-1911)

cloud-loong with the sun and the moon, birds and animals, flowers, birds, fish and insects, landscape, historical allusions and inscriptions of calligraphy and painting. Several sculpture techniques are applied in the production of inkstone, which are circular engraving, deep

中国画与书法

　　中国画又被称为"水墨画",因常用朱红色和青色,所以在古代又被称为"丹青"。中国画是使用毛笔、墨、宣纸、绢帛、砚、颜料等工具和材料进行描绘的,以水墨为主体色,其他颜色为辅助色。中国画以线条为主,来表现物象的形体、气韵和质感。中国画的表现内容和题材主要分为人物、山水和花鸟三大类。人物画表现的是人类社会,山水画表现的是人与自然的关系,花鸟画则表现大自然中的各种生命。三者结合,构成了宇宙的整体,这是中国古人通过艺术表现出来的一种观念和思想,体现出了艺术的真谛。中国画与诗文、书法、篆刻结合,同时,在中国特有的装裱工艺的润色下,具有鲜明、独特的艺术魅力和艺术风格。

　　中国书法是以毛笔书写的、以汉字为基础的一门古老的书写艺术。几千年前,中国人发明了汉字。经过不断的完善和发展,汉字从最早的甲骨文、石鼓文、金文演变为大篆、小篆、隶书,直至定型于草书、楷书、行书等,被艺术性地创造和美化,形成了独特的书法艺术。书法艺术与绘画、诗词结合,共同传达着中国文化的意境,表现出中国传统文化的品格。

Chinese Paining and Calligraphy

The Chinese painting is called ink painting, also known as *Danqing* (*Dan* for the color red, and *Qing* for the color blue) in ancient times people often applied vermilion and cyan colors while drawing. It usually requires writing brush, ink stick, rice paper or silk, inkstone and pigments to accomplish a

- 《黄州寒食帖》 苏轼(宋)

Copybook of Poems Written on Cold Food Festival in Huangzhou, by Su Shi (Song Dynasty, 960-1279)

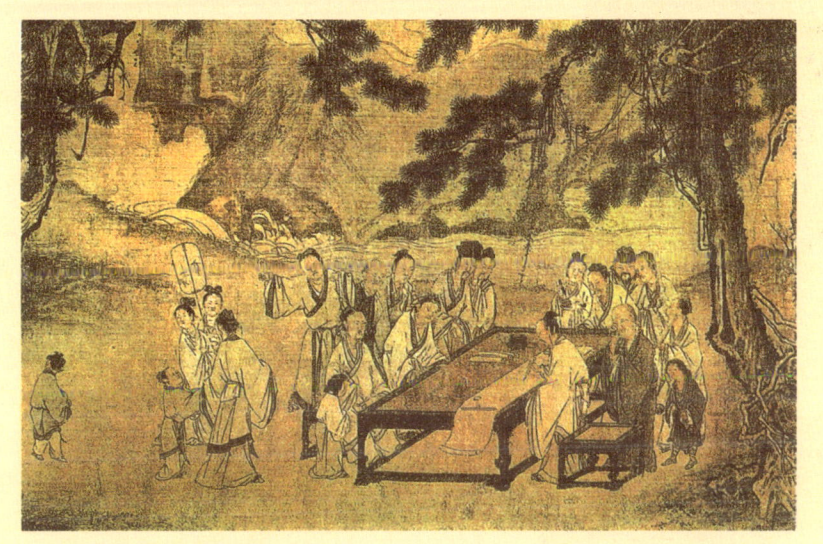

• 绢本水墨画《西园雅集》【局部】 马远（宋）
Ink Painting on Silk: *Elegant Collection of West Garden* [Part], by Ma Yuan (Song Dynasty, 960-1279)

painting which generally takes the ink color as the dominant hue and other colors as the supplement. It mainly uses the lines to express the shape, charm and texture of the object. The content and subject of Chinese painting are generally divided into three categories: figures, landscape and flowers and birds. Figure paintings exhibit human society; landscape paintings present the relationship between man and nature; and flowers and birds paintings display all kinds of creatures in nature. The combination of the three constitutes the entire universe, which is a concept and philosophy expressed through art by ancient Chinese ancestors. It embodies the true essence of the art. Incorporated with literature, calligraphy and seal engraving, as well as the unique Chinese mounting technique, the Chinese painting therefore possesses distinct artistic features.

Chinese calligraphy is an ancient writing art based on Chinese characters and written with writing brush. Thousands of years ago, Chinese people invented Chinese characters which evolved from the early inscriptions on bones or tortoise shells of the Shang Dynasty (1600 B.C.-1046 B.C.) (*Jiaguwen*), inscriptions on drum-shaped stone blocks of the Warring States Period (475 B.C.-221 B.C.)(*Shiguwen*) and inscriptions on ancient bronze objects (*Jinwen*) to large seal script, small seal script and clerical script, and finally to cursive script, regular script and semi-cursive script which are still written at present. They have been artistically created and embellished to form a unique calligraphy. Moreover, it integrates with painting and literature to convey the artistic conception of Chinese culture and present the characteristics of traditional Chinese culture.

• 九龙澄泥砚
Clay (*Chengni*) Inkstone with the Design of Nine Loongs

• "饮中八仙"澄泥砚
Clay (*Chengni*) Inkstone with the Design of the Drunken Eight Immortals

engraving, hollow out engraving, basso-relievo, concave engraving, etc.

Aside from writing brush, ink stick, paper and inkstone, there also appeared several auxiliary appliances, such as vessels used for holding water for ink grind, tools used for placing or dipping writing brush, tools used for pressing rice paper, etc. These appliances are varied according to different functions, like pouring pot, water container, ink box, ink rest, paperweight, pressure bar, manuscript container, brush container, brush holder, brush rack, brush hitch, brush washer, brush dipping, armrest, paper knife, glue rundlet, seal, seal box, copybook holder and writing case, etc. And they are made from various materials including metal, bamboo, wood, porcelain, jade, stone, glass, enamel, lacquer, etc. Those furnishings, with both practical and aesthetic values, are generalized as stationery and bibelot in ancient studies and were cherished by literati and emperors in past dynasties.

故宫懋勤殿

　　懋勤殿是明、清两代的宫殿名,坐落于北京故宫的西南部,是皇帝的书斋,皇帝常在此读书、作诗、赋词、挥毫作画、批阅奏本及鉴赏书画。懋勤之名,取"懋学勤政"之意。懋勤殿在明代建成之初便用来贮藏书籍,清代则"凡图史翰墨之具皆贮焉"。懋勤殿不仅收藏书籍,还藏有历代皇帝御用的书画秘本、法帖、玺印、文房四宝、赏赐记录等。

The Hall of Diligence (*Maoqin Dian*) in the Forbidden City

The name, Hall of Diligence, was used both in the Ming Dynasty (1368-1644) and the Qing Dynasty (1616-1911). It is located in the southwest of the Forbidden City in Beijing, was the study of emperors who could read books, write proses or poems, practice calligraphy or draw Chinese paintings, review submitted memorials as well as appreciate artworks in there. The name *Maoqin* refers to the meaning of diligence. Initially, the Hall of Diligence was built to store books and records in the Ming Dynasty. Later in the Qing Dynasty, its collection covered from books to study appliances. Aside from books, there were secret ancient copies of paintings and calligraphy, inscription rubbings, imperial seals, Scholar's Four Jewels, the record of awards, etc., which were exclusively used by emperors.

- 懋勤殿印盒(清)
  Seal Box in the Hall of Diligence (Qing Dynasty, 1616-1911)

> 文房清供的历史

从河南安阳殷墟的妇好墓和洛阳的西周墓出土的物品来看，早在3000多年前的殷商时代，中国就已经出现了玉制的用于盛放颜料和调色的调色器。

在纸张被发明以前，人们在以竹、木制成的简牍上书写文字，而书刀就是专用于修治简牍的工具。其材

• 牛形玉调色器（西周）（图片提供：FOTOE）
Ox-shaped Jade Palette (Western Zhou Dynasty, 1046 B.C.-771 B.C.)

> History of Stationery and Bibelot in Ancient Studies

According to the articles excavated from the Fuhao Tomb of the Ruins of Yin in Anyang, Henan Province and the tombs of the Western Zhou Dynasty (1046 B.C.-771 B.C.) in Luoyang, Henan Province, we can tell that there already appeared a type of jade palette used for holding pigments and mixing colors dating as far back as the Shang Dynasty (1600 B.C.-1046 B.C.).

Before the birth of paper, people wrote on compiled slips made of bamboo or wood. The book knife is the tool particularly used for revamping the slip, which was made of bronze at an early stage, then iron. A gold embedded iron book knife was unearthed at Tianhui Mountain in Chengdu, Sichuan Province. Gold embedded, also called

竹简（秦）
Bamboo Slips (Qin Dynasty, 221 B.C.-206 B.C.)

gold-and-silver embedded, is a type of craftsmanship: firstly, carve out grooves on the surface of iron ware or bronze ware, then embed gold and silver wires or plaques with the same width into the grooves according to the patterns, and finally burnish the exterior. The excavated book knife has one side inlaid with gold embedded phoenix pattern, and the other side carved with the exact manufacture date: 184 A.D., made by the official workshop of Guanghan in Sichuan Province.

By the Han Dynasty (206 B.C.-220 A.D.), some jade or copper water vessels

质初为青铜，后为铁。四川成都天回山出土过一把错金铁书刀。错金也称"金银错"，就是在铁器或铜器表面刻出沟槽，再按纹样将同样宽度的金银丝、金银片等镶嵌其中，随后磨光表面的工艺。这把书刀的一面嵌有错金的凤纹图案，另一面则錾有确切的制造日期，为公元184年四川广汉官营手工业所造。

汉代出现了玉或铜制的水注、

帛书（汉）
Silk Book (Han Dynasty, 206 B.C.-220 A.D.)

笔洗、砚滴等注水用具，这些早期的文具不仅造型生动、传神，并且具有粗犷、豪放的艺术风格。例如骆驼形的水注，骆驼的身体为空

• 越窑青瓷狮形水注（西晋）
Lion-shaped and Green Glazed Porcelain Pouring Pot from Yue Kiln (Western Jin Dynasty, 265-317)

• 越窑兔形砚滴（三国）
Rabbit-shaped Water Dropper from Yue Kiln (Three Kingdoms Period, 220-280)

has already appeared, such as pouring pot, brush washer and water dropper, etc. These primitive stationery are not only in vivid modeling but also with a rough and bold artistic style. Take the camel-shaped pouring pot as an example: the body of the camel statue has a cavity in which the water can be stored; and at the camelback, there is a hole from which the water can be poured into. If we slightly tilt its body, the water will flow out from the camel's mouth. Additionally, there is a set of stationery excavated from the tombs of the Western Han Dynasty (206 B.C.-25 A.D.) at Phoenix Mountain in Jiangling, Hubei Province, which includes inkstone, writing brush, ink stick, copper knife and blank wooden slips, etc.

The period from the Western Jin Dynasty (265-317) and the Eastern Jin Dynasty (317-420) to the Southern and Northern dynasties (386-589) was an important stage of the development of traditional Chinese culture and art. Under this circumstance, it had a great influence on the improvement of study appliances. In the Jin Dynasty (265-420), appliances like water container, paperweight, brush container, brush lattice, armrest, etc. And porcelain

● 青釉镂空熏炉（西晋）
Green Glazed Hollowed-out Incense Burner (Western Jin Dynasty, 265-317)

● 青釉蛙形水丞（西晋）
Frog-shaped Green Glazed Water Container (Western Jin Dynasty, 265-317)

腔，可盛水，驼背有注水孔，如稍加倾斜，水便会从骆驼口中流出。另外，湖北江陵凤凰山的西汉墓还出土了砚、笔、墨、铜削（铜刀）、无字木牍等整套文具。

stationery has already appeared at this time, which indicates that the application field of the porcelain ware was expanded. In the Yue Kiln, one of the major kilns producing porcelain wares in ancient China, many appliances such as pouring pot, water dropper, water container and brush container were produced. Those articles with plain and simple modeling have solid base and smooth glaze color which is as pure as green jade. There are many proses and poems written to eulogize the study appliance by literati at that time, such as the *Inscription of Terrapin*, by Fu Xuan (Jin Dynasty), the *Ode to Brush Lattice*, by Xiao Gang (emperor of Liang in the Southern and Northern dynasties), and the *Prose of Brush Lattice*, by Wu Yun (historian of Liang in the Southern and Northern dynasties). Besides the detailed description on the texture, function and craftsmanship of these study appliances, they also refer to the arrangement of the stationery in studies.

In the Tang Dynasty(618-907), people started to pay attention to the design of the form, craftsmanship and texture of the study stationery, as well as emphasize the appreciation of the artistic conception and taste expressed by study

• 白釉瓜棱形水丞（唐）
Prismatic Melon Ridges Shaped and White Glazed Water Container (Tang Dynasty, 618-907)

• 三彩莲形笔洗（唐）
Lotus-shaped and Three-color Glazed Brush Washer (Tang Dynasty, 618-907)

　　两晋和南北朝时期是中国古代文化、艺术发展的重要阶段。这种背景对于文房用具的发展也有着重要的影响。晋代时，水丞、镇纸、笔筒、笔格、臂搁等文房器物相继出现，而瓷制的文房用具也开始出现。这表明了瓷器在当时社会生

appliances. Those tools, such as water container, pouring pot and water dropper, paperweight, etc., were fired with three-color glaze, marron glaze, yellow glaze and white glaze, etc., with modelings of duck-shaped, lion-shaped, conch-shaped, melon-shaped, etc. All of them are produced with exquisite style and beautiful colors, possessing a unique feature and reflecting the rich imagination and superb skill of craftsmen at that time.

　　Aside from inheriting the mature manufacturing technique of the precedent dynasties, the study stationery of the Song Dynasty (960-1279) had more varieties, and simple and elegant modeling, possessing a considerably high artistic quality, which not only expanded its practical utility but also raised its value on collection and appreciation. Literati considered stationery and bibelot in ancient studies as a subject of knowledge and wrote plenty of relevant books. Zhao Xihu, the first man in Chinese history who ever compiled and wrote a book about study appliances, enumerated many stationery and illustrated methods of how to identify them one by one, which includes the identifications of inkstone screen, brush lattice, water dropper, etc.,

活中应用范围的扩大。中国古代瓷器生产的主要窑场之一越窑就烧制有水注、砚滴、水丞、笔筒等。这些器物造型古拙，胎质坚硬，釉色莹润，纯净如翠。当时文人写的词赋不少是咏赞文房用具的，如晋代傅玄的《水龟铭》、南朝梁简文帝萧纲的《咏笔格》、南朝梁吴筠的《笔格赋》等。文中除细致地描写了这些文具的材质、用途和制作工艺，还涉及文具在书房中陈设和摆放的位置。

在唐代，人们开始注重文房用具形式、工艺和材质方面的设计，以及对它们表现出的意境及品位的欣赏。这些文房用具，如水丞、水注、砚滴、镇纸等，以三彩釉、酱褐釉、黄釉、白釉等烧制，有鸭形、狮形、海螺形、瓜形等，造型别致，色彩艳丽，可谓匠心独具，反映出当时工匠们丰富的想象力和高超的技艺。

宋代的文房用具在继承前朝成熟的制作技术的基础上，品类更加丰富，艺术性更高，在实用价值得到了拓展的同时，收藏、鉴赏的价值也得到了提升。文人们将文房清供视为一门学问，撰写了许多与

in the *Collection of Dongtian Qinglu*. It also depicts an ideal study in this book and incisively explains the aesthetic function of stationery and bibelot in ancient studies. However in the book, *Illustrations of the Study (Wenfang Tuzan)* by Lin Hong, eighteen different

- 钧窑玫瑰紫釉莲瓣笔洗（宋）
Rose Violet Glazed Brush Washer with Lotus Petals Design from Jun Kiln (Song Dynasty, 960-1279)

- 青白玉兽形砚滴（宋）
Greenish White Jade Water Dropper with Animal Design (Song Dynasty, 960-1279)

• 汝窑笔洗（宋）
Brush Washer from Ru Kiln (Song Dynasty, 960-1279)

• 哥窑五足笔洗（宋）
Five-leg Brush Washer from Ge Kiln (Song Dynasty, 960-1279)

• 白釉瓜形水丞（宋）
White Glazed Ink Water Container Melon Design (Song Dynasty, 960-1279)

study appliances are incarnated into eighteen human beings granted with respective titles and highly praised, like water basin is granted the title of Old Man of Jade Toad.

From the Liao Dynasty (907-1125) to the Yuan Dynasty (1206-1368), it is a period of time of multi-culture fusion. Many study appliances can be found in the tombs of Khitan nobles which were buried along the deceased. And they are handy and portable in order to fit in their nomadic life. The stationery is rich in style and varied in craftsmanship. People constantly innovated and combined all kinds of techniques together, like the animal-shaped paperweight, which is mostly carved by circular engraving: the simple and general way of cutting emphasizes the features of the animal and breathe life in it. And the brush rack of both practicability and esthetics was made in the shape of a continuous mountain. However, by the Yuan Dynasty, the mountain-shaped brush rack had a great difference in its artistic form: it paid attention to symmetrical and regular layout.

In the wake of the cultural prime time of the Ming Dynasty (1368-1644), the stratum of literati started to

文房中的家具——案和博古架

案是一种面板为长方形、下有四足的木制家具。案与桌的不同是，案的腿不在面板的四角之下，而被安装在案两侧向里收进的地方，两侧的案腿间嵌有雕刻着图案的板心和各式券口。书房中用来写字和作画的案分平头案和翘头案。平头案瘦长，案面两端不翘，往往被放在书房的两侧，可摆放文具、书籍，有很浓的书卷气。在平头案的案面两端加上像翘起的飞翼般的翘头，就是翘头案，被陈设在书房内，其上摆放香炉、香薰、花瓶等，显得古雅而静穆。而专供帝王和官吏处理政务和奏章的案叫"奏案"，形制比平头案和翘头案大。

博古架又称"多宝格"，是类似书架的木家具。架子中有高低错落、大小不等的小格，格内可摆放山子、奇石、瓷器等各种古玩，陈设在书房内，可增添典雅气息。

Furniture in Studies: *An* and Antique Shelf

An (narrow long table) is a type of wooden furniture with a rectangular panel and four legs. Other than the table, its four legs are fixed at the slightly inner part along the two sides rather than the four corners of the panel. Two sides of the *An* between the legs are inlaid with planks of carved patterns and various slat frames. The *An* in Chinese studies used for writing and painting, includes flat-end type and upright-end type. The former one is narrow and long,

- 平头案（明）
  Flat-end *An* (Ming Dynasty, 1368-1644)

with flat ends, and is usually placed on the two sides of the study used for exhibiting stationery and books, which has a strong scholar's style. While adding upright ends to the two short sides of the flat-end one, then here we get the upright-end one. It is usually used for displaying incense burner, fragrance, flower vase, etc., conveying an elegant and solemn atmosphere. And the *An* especially used for managing government administration and memorials to the throne by the emperor and officials is called *Zou'an* (*Zou* referring to the memorial to the throne), which is larger than the flat-end and upright-end ones.

The antique shelf is also called Treasure Lattice, which is a type of wooden furniture similar to the book shelf. It is constructed with several little lattices with random arrangement and different sizes, in which it displays rockwork (*Shanzi*), the peculiar rock, porcelain wares and other kinds of antiques in the study to add an elegant ambience.

- 清式博古架（现代）
  Antique Shelf of Qing-dynasty Style (Modern Times)

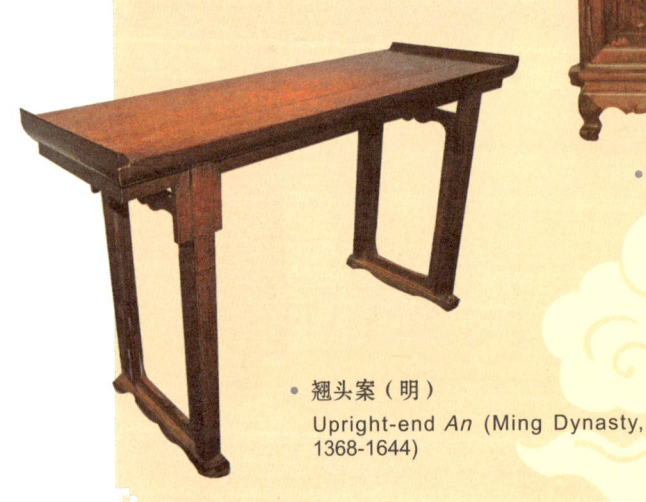

- 翘头案（明）
  Upright-end *An* (Ming Dynasty, 1368-1644)

之相关的书籍。南宋的赵希鹄是中国历史上第一个将文房清供整理出书的人。他在《洞天清禄集》中列举了许多文房用具，并逐个阐明了鉴别方法，有砚屏辨、笔格辨、水滴辨等多项。他还在书中描述出了一个理想化的书房，精辟地道出了文房清供的审美功用。林洪所作的《文房图赞》则把十八种文房用具化为十八个人，并对他们各封了头衔，以文赞之，如将水盂赐号为"玉蜍老翁"。

辽代和元代是一个多元文化相融合的时期。在辽代契丹的贵族墓中经常发现有文房用具随葬，而且所使用的文具都十分轻便，很适宜契丹人的游牧生活。这个时期的文

expand, which forced up the demand for study appliances day by day. The stationery of the Ming Dynasty is of elegance and interest, with the style of pureness, uniqueness, ancientry and profoundness, among which the style of the brush washer is of the richest kinds, mainly including the aquatic plant, melon, fruit and other natural objects. Another category is the imitation of the ancient bronze ware of the Shang Dynasty (1600 B.C.-1046 B.C.), the Zhou Dynasty (1046 B.C.-221 B.C.) and the Han Dynasty (206 B.C.-220A. D.), like the animal-shaped pouring pot which followed the example of the animal-shaped bronze wine cup (*Zun*) of the Shang Dynasty. Aside from the study appliance made of porcelain, jade,

- 白玉荷莲笔洗（明）
  White Jade Brush Washer of Lotus Style (Ming Dynasty, 1368-1644)

• 青玉笔洗（明）
Gray Jade Brush Washer (Ming Dynasty, 1368-1644)

• 青花调色盘（明）
Blue-and-white Palette (Ming Dynasty, 1368-1644)

房清供在造型上更加丰富多彩，在制造工艺上则百花齐放，不断创新，融各种制作技法于一体。如动物形镇纸多以圆雕技法琢制而成，简练而概括的刀法突出了动物的体

copper and ivory, there appeared the one made of lacquer, bamboo, and wood or decorated by enamel and mother-of-pearl inlay, etc. Especially when the masters of bamboo carving who produced abundant classic bamboo brush containers rose successively, they fully revealed the charm of bamboo artwork. Those high-quality study appliances were loved and held in esteem by scholars and became the precious antiques collected by people all over the world. Many literati have written books to comment on stationery and bibelot in ancient studies, which undoubtedly impelled the prosperity of study appliances. According to the book *Kaopan Yushi*, written by Tu Long of the Ming Dynasty, there is one chapter, *Volume of Study Appliances*, which lists 45 common stationery, like pouring pot, water container, washer, ink box, ink rest, paperweight, pressure bar, brush rest, brush boat, brush container, brush holder, brush rack, brush hitch, brush washer, brush dipping, armrest, seal, seal box, paper knife, etc. Under the influence of literati, the royal family put huge financial resources into the study appliances, which turned them from the curio for self-entertainment to the imperial implements. The royal

态特征，显得栩栩如生。集实用与玩赏于一身的笔架，在宋代以前大多被做成与山峰的形制极为相似的连绵状。到了元代，山峰状笔架在艺术形式上已有了很大的不同，大多讲究对称、规整。

明代时，随着文化的进一步繁荣，文人阶层迅速扩大，因此对文房用具的需求与日俱增。明代的文房用具雅趣盎然，在形制上追求清、奇、古、深。其中尤以笔洗的造型最为丰富，以水生植物和瓜果造型为主。另外，还有一类

porcelain stationery made from the royal kiln, Jingdezhen Kiln, Jiangxi Province, is exquisite beyond compare and has almost reached a standard of perfection. As the flourishing of the production of stationery, the social status of folk craftsmen was also raised a lot. The implement made by a prestigious master was usually of higher value.

In the Qing Dynasty (1616-1911), the prevalence and prosperity of study appliances have reached its heyday. The aesthetic idea and the layout system of the study have become a settled life

- 竹雕梅花笔筒（明）
Bamboo Brush Container Carved with Plum Blossoms (Ming Dynasty, 1368-1644)

- 景德镇窑青花山水人物图笔筒（明）
Blue-and-white Brush Container Painted with Landscape and Figures from Jingdezhen Kiln (Ming Dynasty, 1368-1644)

• 青玉兽形水丞（明）
Animal-shaped Green Jade Water Container (Ming Dynasty, 1368-1644)

• 莲式玉水丞（清）
Lotus-shaped Jade Water Container (Qing Dynasty, 1616-1911)

仿制商朝、周朝、汉朝的上古青铜器制成，如牺形水注就效仿了商代的青铜牺尊。文房用具的材质除了陶瓷、玉、铜、象牙等，还增添了漆、竹、木、珐琅、螺钿等。特别在竹刻高手相继出现后，竹制笔筒精品连连问世，充分显示了竹雕的艺术魅力。这些制作精良的文房用

pattern. Meanwhile, the implements have covered almost every category, with more outstanding styles, ornamentation and more skillful production techniques. Especially, when the northwestern area was pacified, the nephrite (*Hetian Jade*) was continuously introduced into the plain area. So many classic jade stationery were made in Suzhou and Yangzhou, including brush container, water container, brush washer, water dropper, inkstone screen, etc. Aside from the carved red technique, the lacquerware stationery also was decorated through the treasure-inlay technique: embedding several precious materials like gemstone, pearl, coral, emerald, agate, ivory and mother-of-pearl in the implements to achieve the effect of magnificence and colorfulness. Some materials including glass, agate, agalwood, etc., were also used to make the study appliances. The most exquisite stationery of the Qing Dynasty was mainly the imperial production, especially the one made by Jingdezhen Kiln in Jiangxi. The pattern was usually drawn by royal painters, with elegant and accurate lines and gorgeous glaze colors, including blue-and-white, five-color, three-color, clashing color, etc. Due to the strong financial support

具受到了文人的喜爱和推崇，成为世人争相收藏的珍玩。文人、学者纷纷著书对文房清供加以评说，这无疑对文房清供的兴盛起到了推动的作用。屠隆所著《考槃余事》一书中有《文房器具笺》一篇，共列举出了45种常用的文房用具，如水注、水丞、水洗、墨盒、墨床、镇纸、压尺、笔床、笔船、笔筒、笔插、笔架、笔挂、笔洗、笔掭、臂搁、印章、印泥盒、纸刀等。受文人影响，皇室更是对文房清供投入了巨大的财力，使文房用具从文人自

of the royal manufacturing department, all talented craftsmen throughout the country were recruited to the imperial palace. In addition to the tributes offered by local administrations, the royal study appliances represented the highest level at that time, such as the royal woodcutting hardwood writing case, in which there are copper paperweight carved with loong motif, lotus-shaped copper brush washer, goat-shaped copper water container, scroll-style copper water container, ox-shaped copper water container, etc. Some of them are even stained by green rust

- 青白玉"九老图"笔筒（清）
Greenish White Jade Brush Container Carved with the *Picture of Nine Old Men* (Qing Dynasty, 1616-1911)

- 青白玉梅花随形笔筒（清）
Greenish White Jade Brush Container Carved with Plum Blossoms (Qing Dynasty, 1616-1911)

娱的文玩进入御用器物一列。江西景德镇官窑烧制的御用陶瓷文房用具精美绝伦，达到了炉火纯青的境界。由于文房用具制作工艺的兴盛发展，民间工匠的社会地位也有了一定的提高，著名工匠所制的器物常常"身价"较高。

　　清代，文房清供的流行和发展达到了鼎盛。文房的审美理念和陈设体系已成为文人定形化了的生活形态。此时，文房用具一应俱全，在形制和纹饰上追求精雅超凡，工艺制作技艺更为纯熟。特别是平定西北之后，和田玉源源不断地进入内地，苏州、扬州等地的工匠制造了很多玉制文具精品，有笔筒、水丞、笔洗、砚滴、砚屏等。漆器文房用具除了用以剔红等雕漆技法，还以百宝嵌的手法进行装饰，将宝石、珍珠、珊瑚、翡翠、玛瑙、象牙、螺钿等一些珍贵材料混合镶嵌在器物上，以达到雍容华贵、五彩缤纷的效果。文房用具的材质中还增添有玻璃、玛瑙、沉香木等。清代文房清供的精品以宫廷制作为主。特别是江西景德镇御窑厂烧制的文房器物，其图案大多出自宫廷画师之手，线条优雅而精确，釉色

• 景德镇窑粉彩人物图笔筒（清）
Famille Rose Brush Container Painted with Figures from Jingdezhen Kiln (Qing Dynasty, 1616-1911)

• 景德镇窑釉里三彩花卉纹笔筒（清）
Underglazed Three-color Brush Container Painted with Floral Pattern from Jingdezhen Kiln (Qing Dynasty, 1616-1911)

艳丽，有青花、五彩、三彩、斗彩等。由于皇家造办处物质力量雄厚，全国各地技艺高超的工匠被征召入内廷，再加上各地的进献，宫廷内的文房用品代表了当时的最高水平。诸如御用硬木雕的文具匣，匣内置有铜螭纹镇纸、铜荷叶笔洗、铜羊形水丞、铜卷书式水丞、铜牛形水丞等器物，并且有些还仿古做以绿色锈迹，反映出清代金石学盛行对文具的影响。

artificially, which reflects the influence of the prevalence of the study of inscriptions in the Qing Dynasty.

金石学

金石学与欧洲的铭刻学近似，是中国考古学的前身，主要研究对象为古铜器和古碑石，尤其是上面的文字铭刻及拓片，还包括竹简、甲骨、玉器、砖瓦、封泥、兵符、明器等，偏重于铭文的著录和考证，以证经补史为研究目的。形成于北宋，至清代正式被称为"金石之学"。金石学保存了很多有价值的铭文资料，考证出了不少古器物的名称和用途。

The Study of Inscriptions

The study of inscriptions is very similar to the epigraphy in Europe, which is the predecessor of archaeology in China, focusing on the research of ancient bronze or copper wares and the stone tablet, especially the inscription and rubbing of the carved characters on them. Others include bamboo slip, oracle bone, jade ware, brick tile, seal mud, commander's tally and funerary object, etc. This subject lays particular stress on the record and textual verification of inscriptions to provide evidence for history study. It formed in the Northern Song Dynasty (960-1127), and was formally called the study of inscriptions in the Qing Dynasty. It has helped to preserve many valuable inscription materials and find out the actual name and function of abundant ancient implements.

030

文房清供
Stationery and Bibelot in Ancient Studies

● 书桌一角（图片摄佛，今贤正片）
A Corner of the Desk

文房清供的品类
Categorization of Stationery and Bibelot in Ancient Studies

文房清供品类繁多，不胜枚举。本章按照文具与笔、墨、纸、砚的相关性对文房用具进行分类。

There are too numerous categories of the stationery and bibelot in ancient studies to mention one by one. This chapter sorts them according to their relationship with writing brush, ink stick, paper and inkstone.

> 与笔相关的文房用具

笔架

笔架是随着毛笔的使用而被创造出来的，被摆放在书案上用于放笔或架笔。由于毛笔呈圆管状，在桌上易于滚动，又因笔头上沾有墨汁会弄脏其他物品，笔架是文房中少不了的用具之一。笔架还有"笔山""笔规""笔悬"等称谓。南朝时，笔架被称为"笔床"，徐陵

- 粉彩笔床（清）
Famille Rose Porcelain Brush Rest (Qing Dynasty, 1616-1911)

> Study Appliances Associated with Writing Brush

Brush Rack

The brush rack was created along with the usage of writing brush. It can be seen on the table for placing or holding the brush. As the penholder is a circular tube which makes it easily roll around, and the ink dipped at the tip of the brush sometimes stains other objects, the brush rack is a necessary tool in the study. It also can be called brush mountain, brush regulation, brush hang, etc. In the Southern dynasties (420-589), the brush rack was called brush rest, which is mentioned in the poem, *Yutai Xinyong Xu*, by Xu Ling: the color-glazed inkstone case, I shall carry it with me all day long; wthe emerald brush rest, I shall never let it out of my reach. In the Yuan Dynasty (1206-1368), it was called brush lattice, which is recorded in the *Biography of Buhumu, History of*

• 笔架的使用方法
Usage of Brush Rack

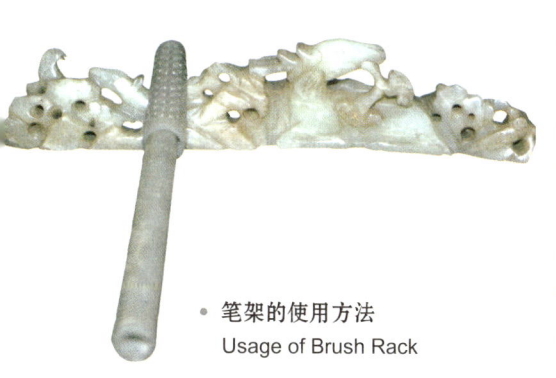

的《玉台新咏序》一文中有"琉璃砚匣，终日随身；翡翠笔床，无时离手"之句。元代又称之为"笔格"，《元史·不忽木传》记载：大臣不忽木因功"受沉水假山、象牙镇纸、水晶笔格"。中国最早的笔架实物是江苏无锡的北宋中期墓葬出土的影青瓷兽形笔架水注，这是笔架与水注一体的两用器物。

笔架没有固定形状，只要保持毛笔固定并悬空的状态即可。笔架以山形最为常见，有三峰、五峰、十二峰等形式，峰峦横列，峰与峰之间有弧形"山坳"，作搁笔之用。笔架的材质有玉、铜、铁、水晶、紫砂、陶瓷、象牙、玛瑙、琥珀、珐琅、木等多种。奇形怪状的石头如被取其自然形态，也可作为笔架，如小巧

the Yuan Dynasty: the official Buhumu was granted the sink rockwork, ivory paperweight, and crystal brush lattice due to his merits and achievements. The earliest brush rack preserved by now is the animal-shaped greenish white porcelain brush rack pouring pot excavated from the tombs of the middle age of the Northern Song Dynasty (960-1127) in Wuxi, Jiangsu Province. It is a special object having the dual purpose of brush rack and pouring pot.

The brush rack doesn't have a fixed style; as long as it can settle the writing brush and keep it hanging in the air. The most regular one is the mountain-shaped style. It includes several styles like the three-peak, the five-peak and the twelve-peak, etc. The col and peak are arranged in a horizontal line. And the lower part is used to place the writing brush. The materials people used to make the brush includes jade, copper, iron, crystal, purple sands, porcelain, ivory, agate, amber, enamel and wood, etc. Sometimes the natural stone of peculiar shapes also can be used as a brush rack, like the exquisite *Lingbi* Stone, *Ying* Stone, etc. The typical characteristic of brush rack is small. Besides its practical function, it can be played in hands.

- 青玉鹿纹笔架（明）
Green Jade Brush Rack with Deer Pattern
(Ming Dynasty, 1368-1644)

There is another rare and unique tool for placing writing brush called brush boat. It has a boat-like appearance: narrow base and wide mouth, in which a mountain-shaped block cut it out at one third point of the brush boat. Then the brush can be placed on the block.

- 水晶灵芝笔架（清）
Ganoderma-shaped Crystal Brush Rack
(Qing Dynasty, 1616-1911)

- 象牙挂笔架（现代）
Ivory Brush Hitch (Modern Times)

的灵璧石、英石等。笔架的典型特征是小巧，不仅实用，还可被拿在手里把玩。

另外，还有一种少见而特殊的置笔用具，称为"笔船"，形为下窄上宽的船形，"船"内三分之一处有山峰形的隔断，可将毛笔搁置其中。

- 青花笔船（明）
Blue-and-white Brush Boat (Ming Dynasty, 1368-1644)

- 铜笔山（宋）
Copper Brush Mountain (Song Dynasty, 960-1279)

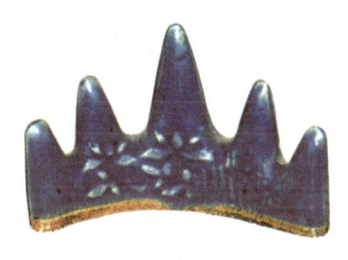

- 青花五峰笔山（清）
Blue-and-white Five-peak Brush Mountain (Qing Dynasty, 1616-1911)

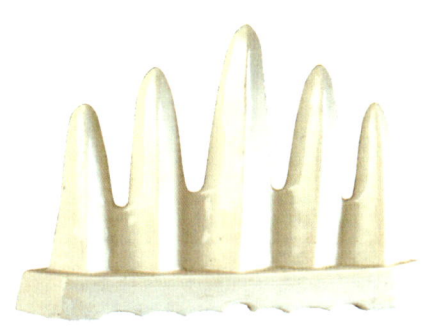

- 白瓷笔架（明）
White Porcelain Brush Rack (Ming Dynasty, 1368-1644)

- 黑釉笔山（明）
Black Glazed Brush Mountain (Ming Dynasty, 1368-1644)

笔筒

笔筒是盛装毛笔的器具，将毛笔的笔锋朝上插装在其内。因其形状为筒形，故称"笔筒"。笔筒的造型很简单，多直口、直壁，上下同宽、同形，以圆筒形为主，此外还有方形、多角形、梅花形、云头形等。笔筒在东晋时期已出现，在

Brush Container

The brush container is a tool used for storing the writing brushes. Brushes should be placed in it with their tip heading upwards. As it has a cylindrical appearance, it is called brush container (*Bitong*). It has a simple style, mostly with a straight mouth and wall. The two ends usually have the same shape.

• 青釉笔筒（晋）
Green Glazed Brush Container
(Jin Dynasty, 265-420)

• 蓝上蓝福寿墨彩花鸟纹海棠式笔筒（清）
Double Layer Blue Brush Container Painted with Framed Chinese Painting of Flowers and Birds in the Theme of Good Fortune and Longevity (Qing Dynasty, 1616-1911)

Besides the cylindrical style, there are several other intersections like square, polygon, quincunx, cloud-head, etc. The brush container appeared no later than the Eastern Jin Dynasty (317-420). According to *Zhixu Ge Zazu* of the Song Dynasty (960-1279), Wang Xizhi (great calligraphy master in the Jin Dynasty) took a peculiar stone as his brush rack, named *Huban*; Wang Xianzhi (great calligraphy master in the Jin Dynasty) had a mottled bamboo brush container named *Qiuzhong*. The two appliances are unrivalled in the world. The brush container is mostly made of porcelain. By the Eastern Jin Dynasty, there appeared the green glazed one. Then other types emerged successively like the blue-and-white, polychrome, famille rose, three-color, clashing color, ink color, gold traced, single color-glazed and enamel porcelain brush containers. Besides the porcelain one, there are many containers made of bamboo, wood, ivory, jade, lacquer and calabash. According to the *Compile of Stationery* written by Tu Long of the Ming Dynasty (1368-1644), the elegant brush container usually is made of mottled bamboo, with red sandalwood or ebony inlaid prismatic mouth. Others will not be accounted for. By the middle

- 五彩人物笔筒（清）
  Polychrome Brush Container Painted with Figures (Qing Dynasty, 1616-1911)

- 粉彩花卉纹墨书御题诗纹六角形笔筒（清）
  Hexagon Prism Famille Rose Brush Container Painted with Flowers and Inscription (Qing Dynasty, 1616-1911)

- 红彩描金云蝠纹卷书式笔筒（清）
  Scroll-shaped Gold-traced Red Porcelain Brush Container with Cloud and Bat Patterns (Qing Dynasty, 1616-1911)

- 青玉雕水仙花笔筒（清）
  Green Jade Brush Container Carved with Daffodil Pattern (Qing Dynasty, 1616-1911)

• 竹雕笔筒（清）
Bamboo Carving Brush Container (Qing Dynasty, 1616-1911)

• 景德镇窑仿竹刻夔纹笔筒（清）
Bamboo Imitation Porcelain Brush Container with Loong Pattern from Jingdezhen Kiln (Qing Dynasty, 1616-1911)

宋代《致虚阁杂俎》中载："羲之有巧石笔架，名'扈班'，献之有斑竹笔筒，名'裘钟'，皆世无其匹。"讲的是晋代的大书法家王羲之和王献之各有一件举世无双的文房用具：王羲之有用奇石制成的名为"扈班"的笔架，王献之有用斑竹制作的名为"裘钟"的笔筒。笔筒的材质以陶瓷为多，东晋时出现了青釉笔筒，后来历代还陆续出现了青花、五彩、粉彩、三彩、斗彩、墨彩、描金、单色釉、画珐琅等陶瓷笔筒。除了陶瓷，笔筒还多

age of the Ming Dynasty, a bunch of skillful craftsmen appeared. They can carve exquisite brush containers out of the plain bamboo. Some are simple and elegant; some are delicate and exquisite. They all became people's favorite classic study appliances.

There is another study appliance called brush holder, made of jade, crystal, stone, etc., having many peculiar styles, which is different from the regular container.

以竹、木、象牙、玉、漆、匏等制成。明代屠隆的《文具雅编》载："笔筒，湘竹为之，以紫檀、乌木棱口镶座为雅，余不入品。"明代中叶以后，涌现出了一批能工巧匠，能将光素无纹的竹子雕制成精美的笔筒。这些竹笔筒有的古朴而典雅，有的雕镂剔透，成为备受人们喜爱的文房精品。

还有一种插笔的文房用具叫"笔插"，材质有玉、水晶、石等。与形制规整的笔筒不同，笔插的形状千奇百怪。

• 紫晶笔插（清）
Amethyst Brush Holder (Qing Dynasty, 1616-1911)

笔筒上的图案

笔筒上的图案内容极为广泛，有自然风景、人物、动物、花鸟等，几乎无所不包。不过受书画和文学的影响，其图案题材是有所偏重的。如书画中常见的表现文人气节的岁寒三友图，表现文人相聚的竹林七贤图、松荫高士图、山水人物图，以及仕女图、泛舟图、狩猎图、牧牛图、渔家乐图等在笔筒上较为常见。马的题材在笔筒上也出现得较多，有相马、沈马、喂马、奔马等，这是因为马有飘逸、潇洒的气质，为文人所喜爱。另外还有表现松、鹤、四季花卉等有着吉祥寓意的图案。

Patterns on the Brush Container

The pattern on the brush container is varied in content, including natural landscape, figures, animals, flowers and birds. However, under the influence of Chinese painting, calligraphy and literature, the theme of the container has its unique preference, including the common one—three durable plants of winter, several ones with the theme of literati's get-together—the seven sage in bamboo forest, the master in the pine shade, landscape and figures, as well as the portrait of a lady, picture of rowing a boat, picture of hunting, picture of ox-herding and picture of fishing, etc. Horses also appear frequently on the brush container, like identifying horse, bathing horse, feeding horse, galloping on horse, etc. It is because the horse possesses the quality of elegance and gracefulness, which is loved by scholars. Additionally, there are auspicious patterns like pine, crane and flowers of the four seasons. It has helped to preserve many valuable inscription materials and find out the actual name and function of abundant ancient implements.

- 竹雕山水人物笔筒（清）
Bamboo Brush Container Carved with Landscape and Figures (Qing Dynasty, 1616-1911)

- 彩绘动物花瓣笔筒（清）
Colored Porcelain Brush Container Painted with Animal and Petals (Qing Dynasty, 1616-1911)

- 翡翠松鹤延年笔筒（近代）
Emerald Brush Container Carved with Pine and Crane (Modern Times)

- 竹雕松树笔筒（清）
Bamboo Brush Container Carved with Pines (Qing Dynasty, 1616-1911)

笔洗

笔洗是洗涮毛笔的一种用具。用毛笔蘸墨写字时，因为墨中含胶，墨干后会把毛笔笔头的毛粘住，待再用水泡开时，会损伤笔头。所以在暂时不用毛笔时，一定在笔洗中将它洗涮干净。另外，在画中国画时，因为要时时改变墨色和颜色的深浅，也要随时洗毛笔。所以，笔洗也是文房中不可缺少的用具。

笔洗开口大，便于涮笔。根据毛笔的大小，笔洗也有大小之分，而且造型各异；材质有玉、金属、竹、陶瓷、象牙、珐琅、玻璃等。笔洗约出现在秦、汉两代，汉代有岫岩青玉制的笔洗，口、足呈圆形，内空，可储水。在现存的传世瓷笔洗中，最早的是宋代汝窑和钧窑的制品。内蒙古敖汉旗辽代墓葬曾出土有银笔洗，说明当时的契丹人也喜好文墨。明代时，有着长寿之意的桃式笔洗也极为盛行。桃式笔洗的器形如一只半剖的桃子，可盛水，外壁的镂雕枝叶为把手，枝叶向下弯曲，并延伸至底部，形成底足。陶瓷笔洗则在各色釉地上饰

Brush Washer

The brush washer is a tool used for washing the writing brush. While writing, the brush tip will stick together after the ink dries out, as the ink contains glue. Later, when people soak the brush in water to wash out the glue, it will injure the tip. So the brush should be washed cleanly when not in use. Besides, in Chinese painting, as the ink color and the shade of the pigment need to be changed from time to time, the brush also needs to be washed accordingly. So the brush washer is a necessary tool in the study.

The brush washer usually has a large mouth, which is convenient for washing

- 粉彩青花三童笔洗（清）
Three-child Style Famille Rose Brush Washer (Qing Dynasty, 1616-1911)

• 松石绿釉夔龙纹笔洗（清）
Turquoise Green Glazed Porcelain Brush Washer Carved with Loong Pattern (Qing Dynasty, 1616-1911)

• 天蓝釉笔洗（清）
Azure Glazed Brush Washer (Qing Dynasty, 1616-1911)

• 粉青釉腰圆式笔洗（清）
Pinkish Green Glazed Brush Washer with a Bulging Waist (Qing Dynasty, 1616-1911)

brushes. According to the size of the brush, the washer is also varied in size and style. The common materials include jade, metal, bamboo, porcelain, ivory, enamel, glass, etc. The brush washer appeared in the Qin Dynasty (221 B.C.-206 B.C.) and the Han Dynasty. The gray jade washer from Xiuyan in the Han Dynasty has a round mouth and foot, with a hollowed body that can store water. Among the existing porcelain brush washers, the earliest one was made in Ru Kiln and Jun Kiln in the Song Dynasty. And the silver brush washer once was excavated from the tombs of the Liao Dynasty (907-1125) in Aohan County, Inner Mongolia, which indicates that Khitan people were also fond of calligraphy. By the Ming Dynasty, the peach-shaped brush washer which carries the meaning of longevity started to prevail. It looks like a half peach and can store water. The hollow engraved branches and leaves attached to the exterior can be used as its handle; and the branches extending to the bottom can be seen as its foot. As to the porcelain brush washer, people decorate dark flowers or apply pigments to draw several patterns on the glaze of different colors. The style of the washer in the Qing Dynasty (1616-

有暗花，或加彩作图案。清代的笔洗造型更加多彩，有葡萄叶式、海棠式、楸叶式、荷叶式等，叶形微卷，如掌，纳水其中，即成笔洗。

1911) varies in many kinds, like the grape leaf style, crabapple style, Chinese catalpa leaf style, lotus leaf style, etc. The leaf-shaped one curls a little and is the same size as human's palm, which can be used as brush washer when it is filled with water.

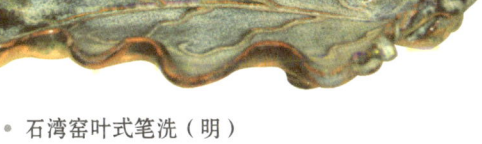

- 石湾窑叶式笔洗（明）
Leaf-shaped Brush Washer from Shiwan Kiln (Ming Dynasty, 1368-1644)

- 景德镇窑仿汝窑桃式笔洗（清）
Peach-shaped Brush Washer with the Style of Ru Kiln, from Jingdezhen Kiln (Qing Dynasty, 1616-1911)

- 乾隆款仿哥窑楸叶笔洗（清）
Chinese Catalpa Leaf-shaped Brush Washer with the Style of Ge Kiln, Stamped by Characters of Qianlong (Qing Dynasty, 1616-1911)

- 青玉灵芝笔洗（清）
Ganoderma-shaped Green Jade Brush Washer (Qing Dynasty, 1616-1911)

- 白玉荷花笔洗（清）
Lotus-shaped White Jade Brush Washer (Qing Dynasty, 1616-1911)

- 青玉福寿花形笔洗（清）
Flower-shaped Green Jade Brush Washer with the Theme of Good Fortune and Longevity (Qing Dynasty, 1616-1911)

- 青玉秋蝉桐叶笔洗（清）
Green Jade Brush Washer with the Design of Autumn Cicada and Chinese Parasol Leaf (Qing Dynasty, 1616-1911)

- 仿古云龙纹玉笔洗（清）
Ancient Style Jade Brush Washer Carved with Cloud and Loong Patterns (Qing Dynasty, 1616-1911)

- 白玉螭纹葫芦式笔洗（清）
Calabash-shaped White Jade Brush Washer Carved with Loong Pattern (Qing Dynasty, 1616-1911)

笔掭

　　笔掭是用以理顺毛笔的笔毫或用以验墨的浓淡的器具，以避免下笔之时在一笔之间发生的墨色浓淡不均的现象。笔掭又称"笔覗""笔填""笔舔"等。用于制作笔掭的材料的颜色都很浅，而且质地细密，这样既便于辨认墨色的浓淡、深浅是否合度，也不会吸附墨汁，使用过后便于用水清洗。

　　在明代屠隆所著的《考槃余事》中列举的四十五种文房器具中，笔掭排在第八位，可见它在当时的文人心目中的地位。笔掭大约在宋代出现，明代文震亨的《长物志》中有"笔覗"的条目："笔覗，定窑、龙泉小浅碟俱佳，水晶、琉璃诸式俱不雅，有玉碾片叶为之者，尤俗。"可知当时的笔覗是小浅碟，叶片造型，材质有陶瓷、水晶、琉璃、玉石、象牙等，其中尤以龙泉窑、定窑的瓷笔掭为最好。笔掭虽小，但在工艺制作上仍被采用了浮雕、圆雕、镂雕、线刻等多种技法，造型轻灵而剔透，充满灵性。

　　砚石亦可作为笔掭的材质，如

Brush Dipping

The brush dipping is used to comb the writing brush or test the ink shade, in order to keep the color consistency. It is also called brush survey (*Bichan*), brush filler, brush lick, etc. The materials used to produce the brush dipping are all in a light color and compact texture, which is convenient for identifying the color shade without absorbing the ink. And it is easy to wash after use.

　　In the book *Kaopan Yushi*, written by Tu Long of the Ming Dynasty, among the listed 45 study appliances, the brush dipping ranks in the eighth position, which indicates its importance in literati's mind. The brush dipping approximately appeared in the Song Dynasty. And it is

- 景德镇窑仿官窑笔掭（清）
Brush Dipping with Royal Style from Jingdezhen Kiln (Qing Dynasty, 1616-1911)

砚石中的名品端石和歙石。其造型也由原先的浅碟状变成不经雕琢的砚式素面状。以这类砚石制成的笔掭称为"仔砚"，其观赏价值和收藏价值往往高于实用价值。

mentioned in the *Superfluous Things*, by Wen Zhenheng of the Ming Dynasty: as to the brush dipping, the best one is the small saucer made from the Ding Kiln and Longquan Kiln. The one made of crystal and colored glaze is vulgar. And the one made of jade and carved in leaf-shape is of the coarsest. So we know that the brush dipping is like a small saucer, with the leaf style, and made of porcelain, crystal, colored glaze, jade, ivory, etc. And the porcelain made from Longquan Kiln and Ding Kiln is of the best quality. Although it is in small size, the brush dipping is still carved through several techniques including basso-relievo, circular engraving, hollow engraving and linellae carving, which forms an exquisite and inspiring style.

- 定窑白釉"官"字款划花荷叶式笔掭（五代）
Lotus Leaf Style White Glazed Brush Dipping with 官 (*Guan*)'s Pattern from Ding Kiln (Five Dynasties, 907-960)

- 绿釉叶形笔掭（清）
Leaf-shaped Green Glazed Brush Dipping (Qing Dynasty, 1616-1911)

The inkstone also can be used to make brush dipping, like the famous *Duan* stone and *She* stone. Accordingly, its style is changed from the former small saucer to the plain inkstone style. Such a kind of brush dipping made of inkstone is called little inkstone (*Ziyan*), which usually possesses higher aesthetic value and collection value than its practical function.

笔匣

笔匣就是盛放毛笔的匣子，是用来贮存新笔的，有的笔匣中放有药物，以防蛀蚀。据文献记载，汉代就已经有了笔匣。《西京杂记》中载："天子笔以杂宝为匣，侧以玉璧、翠羽，皆直百金。"清代陈元龙的《格致镜原》中的《文具四·笔匣》载："汉末，一笔之匣，雕以黄金，饰以和璧，缀以隋珠，文以翡翠。"并说："宋徽宗陵内有走花鸟、玉笔箱。"从笔匣的奢华程度，可见当时的帝王，以及文人、雅士对毛笔的重视程度。笔匣的材料有玉、金属、雕漆、描金漆、紫檀、楠木、文竹、掐丝珐琅等，形制大多为长方形，子母口，内附一屉，或为双层。

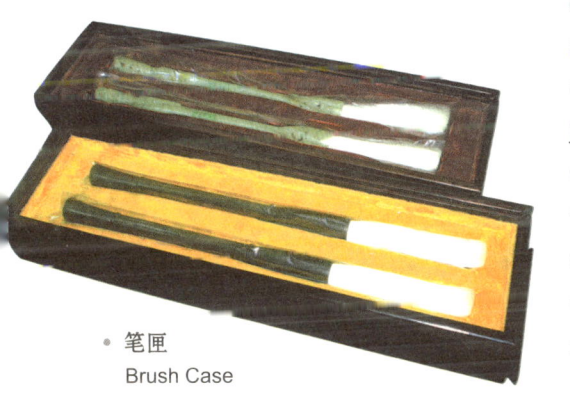

- 笔匣
Brush Case

Brush Case

The brush case is used to store the new writing brushes. Sometimes, people put herbs in it to avoid the damage by worms. According to the record, there appeared the brush case in the Han Dynasty. In the book *Notes of the Western Capital*, it depicts that the emperor's brushes are stored in gem embedded case; the case is decorated with circular jade and a kingfisher's feather on two sides. So the case is invaluable. According to the chapter *Stationery: Brush Case* of the book *Gezhi Jingyuan* written by Chen Yuanlong of the Qing Dynasty, by the end of the Han Dynasty, the brush case was decorated with gold, circular jade, gem bead and emerald; and there is jade brush case carved with flower and bird patterns found in the tomb of Emperor Huizong of the Song Dynasty. From the extravagance of the case, we can see how much the emperor and literati value the writing brush. The brush case is made of jade, metal, carved lacquerware, gold-traced lacquerware, red sandalwood, *Nan* wood, asparagus fern, filigree enamel, etc., with the style of rectangle, son-and-mother mouth. Some might have an inside drawer or double-deck.

> 与墨相关的文房用具

墨床

墨床是用来放置墨锭的小器具。在研墨过程中稍事停歇时，墨锭的一头往往带有墨汁，为防止墨汁污损书案和纸张，所以要有地方搁置墨锭，而这供临时搁放墨锭的器具因形状如床而得名为"墨床"，亦称"墨架""墨台"。墨床的造型多为几案式或床式，还有的被做成书卷式、多宝格式；往往下有四足，上面还雕有各种纹饰，有些还配有硬木座。但不论形状如何，墨床通常不会太大，宽不过5厘米，长不过9厘米，小巧玲珑；材质有铜、玉、木、陶瓷、漆、琥珀、玛瑙、翡翠、珐琅、玻璃、象牙等。

最早记载墨床的文献出现在明

> Study Appliances Associated with Ink Stick

Ink Rest

The ink rest is used for placing ink stick. While grinding the ink stick, as the stick is stained with ink on one side, it needs to be placed on the ink rest to avoid smearing the table or paper. The ink rest gets the name as it looks like a bed, also called ink rack or ink stand. It is usually made in the table style or bed style. Some are made in the scroll style, and treasure slot style. It mainly has four feet at the bottom and is carved with various patterns on the above. Some might be equipped with hardwood seats. The ink rests are generally produced in small and exquisite sizes, with a width of 5 cm and a length of 9 cm at the most. The materials include copper, jade, wood, porcelain, lacquer, amber, agate, emerald, enamel, glass, ivory, etc.

- 黄玛瑙竹节式墨床（清）
Bamboo Style Yellow Agate Ink Rest (Qing Dynasty, 1616-1911)

- 白玉俎式墨床（清）
Chopping Block Style White Jade Ink Rest (Qing Dynasty, 1616-1911)

- 水晶墨床（清）
Crystal Ink Rest (Qing Dynasty, 1616-1911)

- 粉彩墨床（清）
Famille Rose Ink Rest (Qing Dynasty, 1616-1911)

代。由于明代制墨业繁盛，墨床也随之流行。因当时的社会崇尚古朴之风，故墨床的外形常与墨的外形相吻合，线条劲挺，棱角分明，往往通体不加任何雕饰。清代是雅玩文房的鼎盛期，墨床也从单纯的承墨用具发展到既实用，又可赏玩的艺术品。墨床的用材更加多样化，纹饰也更加繁复、华丽，装饰技法有镶嵌、镂雕、浮雕、描金等。清

The earliest record of the ink rest is in the Ming Dynasty (1368-1644). Due to the prosperity of the ink stick production, the ink rest was in prevalence accordingly. As people were fond of the simple and plain style, the appearance of ink rest and ink stick usually fitted with each other, with vigorous linellae and clear edges, without any decoration. The Qing Dynasty (1616-1911) is the heyday of the study appliance. The ink

代的墨床设计巧妙，工艺到位，典雅而华丽，极富装饰性。

墨盒

顾名思义，墨盒就是盛放墨汁的盒子。墨盒以铜制和锡制的为多，里面放有丝绵。将墨汁倒入盒中后，让墨汁浸到丝绵中，然后用毛笔蘸墨以书写。墨盒内的墨汁不会干涸、变质，比用砚台研墨方便很多。墨盒出现得较晚，大约在清嘉庆或道光年间。其形制多为正方形或圆形，上面刻有图案和文字，十分典雅。

• 铜墨盒（清）
Copper Ink Box (Qing Dynasty, 1616-1911)

rest also developed from the ink stick bearing tool to a type of artwork with practical and aesthetic values. Besides the diversification of its material, the motif also turned out to be more extravagant. The decoration techniques include inlay, hollow engraving, basso-relievo, gold trace, etc. It has a delicate design, skillful craftsmanship as well as elegant and graceful feature.

Ink Box

The ink box, as its name implies, is a tool for storing ink, mostly made of copper and tin, with silk floss placed inside. After people put ink into the box, let the silk floss soak with it, and then use a brush to dip the ink absorbed on the floss while writing. The ink stored in the ink box will not dry out or go bad. And it is more convenient than grinding the ink stick. The ink box approximately appeared in the Period of Jiaqing and Daoguang in the Qing Dynasty (1796-1850). With the regular style of square or round, some might be carved with patterns and inscriptions, which make them elegant and graceful.

> 与纸相关的文房用具

裁刀

　　裁刀是割裂纸张的一种工具，也叫"纸刀"。明代文震亨《长物志》载："有古刀笔，青绿裹身，上尖下圆，长仅尺许，用以杀青为书，今入入文具似雅……"最初的裁刀也作他用，后为裁纸所专用。因为它较钝，所以主要用来裁书画用的毛边纸、宣纸等。其材料有铜、象牙、竹、紫檀等。裁刀的制作工艺和用材考究，往往刀柄及刀

• 象牙纸刀（清）
Ivory Paper Knife (Qing Dynasty, 1616-1911)

> Study Appliances Associated with Paper

Paper Knife

The paper knife is a tool used to cut papers, also called cutting shear. According to the *Superfluous Things* written by Wen Zhenheng in the Ming Dynasty (1368-1644), the ancient paper knife was covered in green color, having a sharp tip and round handle, with a length of 1/3 meter, which was used to make the bamboo slip in the old time. Nowadays, people see it as a type of stationery. The earliest paper knife also had other functions. Later, it was used to cut the paper exclusively. As the blade is blunt, it is mainly for cutting the feather edge paper, rice paper, etc. The paper knife is made of copper, ivory, bamboo, red sandalwood, etc. The craftsmanship and material are carefully chosen: the knife handle and sheath are made of

鞘为竹或紫檀制，刀身为象牙制，刀柄及刀鞘镶嵌有象牙、宝石等装饰物，鞘上还带有鎏金小环。

镇纸

镇纸是用于镇压书页或纸张的器具，又名"书镇""文镇"等。在纸上写字、作画时，很忌讳纸张不平整，用镇纸压住纸张的一端，把纸抻平，便于书写。镇纸在南北朝时就已经出现，《南史·垣护之传》载："帝尝以书案下安鼻为楯，以铁为书镇如意，甚壮大，以备不虞，欲以代杖。"以铁做的镇纸又重，又大，被放在书房中还可以作为护身之器，以备不时之需。镇纸在宋代还有"千钧史""套子龟""小连城"等别称。 明代，有

• 紫檀木嵌竹刻镇纸（现代）
Bamboo Carving Inlaid Rosewood Paperweight (Modern Times)

bamboo or red sandalwood; the knife blade is made of ivory. The knife handle and sheath are inlaid with ivory and gemstones, etc. Sometimes, the sheath is equipped with a little gilded ring.

Paperweight

The paper weight is used to press the book pages or papers, also called book weight, writing weight, etc. While writing or painting on the paper, it is crucial to keep the paper neat. So people usually press one end of the paper with paperweight to keep it flat. It is convenient for writing. The paperweight appeared in the Southern and Northern Dynasties (420-589). According to the *History of the South*, the emperor once set a shield under the table and used the iron as paperweight. The paperweight made of iron is heavy and large, which can be used as a weapon in case of need. In the Song Dynasty (960-1127), it was also called *Qianjunshi*, *Taozigui*, *Xiaoliancheng*, etc. In the Ming Dynasty, some paperweight with the shape of a ruler was usually called book ruler, press ruler and weight ruler. It has the same function as the paperweight. The paperweight in the Qing Dynasty (1616-1911) was delicate and exquisite, such as the ivory carving

• 白玉镇尺（清）
White Jade Weight Ruler (Qing Dynasty, 1616-1911)

• 青玉镇尺（清）
Green Jade Weight Ruler (Qing Dynasty, 1616-1911)

• 白玉雕龙镇纸（清）
White Jade Paperweight Carved with a Loong (Qing Dynasty, 1616-1911)

paperweight with the design of a pine tree: it is carved as a pine tree. At the bottom, there is a hidden design. An oval water container is placed under the lid.

The paperweight is mainly made of heavy materials. Besides iron, copper, jade, stone, agate, crystal and porcelain ones, the glass, enamel, ivory, bamboo and wood are also can be used to make paperweight. It has an elegant style and strong decorative features, mostly with the design of precious animals such as toad, tiger, *Chi*, dog, *Pixie*, lion, hare, ox, horse, deer, sheep, bear, etc. The linellae is vivid and life-like. Additionally, there are the ones with the style of bamboo and zither. Paperweights have several basic features, a flat bottom, a low barycenter

些长方形类似尺子的镇纸也常被称作"书尺""压尺"或"镇尺"，其功用与镇纸相同。清代的镇纸制作精美，如故宫中的一件象牙雕松树镇纸，为松干状，下部的松针处有一处机关，拉动可掀起一盖，盖下是椭圆形的水丞，可一物多用。

镇纸都是以较重的材质制作而成的，除了铁、铜、玉、石、玛

• 铜狮镇纸（清）
Copper Lion Paperweight (Qing Dynasty, 1616-1911)

瑙、水晶、陶瓷，还有玻璃、珐琅、象牙、竹、木等材质。镇纸造型古雅，装饰性强，以异兽及动物居多，有蟾蜍、虎、螭、犬、辟邪、狮、兔、牛、马、鹿、羊、熊等，纹饰生动而逼真。另外，还有竹节古琴等造型的镇纸。不论镇纸的造型如何，都具有底部平整、重心低、有一定重量这几个基本特点。镇纸上往往还开有小孔，可系绳，便于携带，是集实用和观赏于一体的文房器物。

and a heavy weight. The weight sometimes is pierced with little holes for stringing thread while being carried along. It is a study appliance with both practical function and aesthetic value.

- 白玉牛形镇纸（清）
  White Jade Ox Paperweight (Qing Dynasty, 1616-1911)

- 白玉"榴开百子"镇纸（清）
  White Jade Paperweight with the Theme of Pomegranate Bearing Hundreds of Seeds (Qing Dynasty, 1616-1911)

- 象牙刻唐诗镇尺（清）
  Ivory Carving Weight Ruler Carved with Poem Inscriptions (Qing Dynasty, 1616-1911)

- 青玉天鹅形镇纸（清）
  Green Jade Swan Paperweight (Qing Dynasty, 1616-1911)

- 青玉"三阳开泰"镇纸（清）
Green Jade Paperweight with the Theme of Auspicious Beginning of a New Year (Qing Dynasty, 1616-1911)

- 翡翠双莲镇纸（清）
Emerald Paperweight with the Design of Double-lotus (Qing Dynasty, 1616-1911)

螭与辟邪

螭是中国古代神话中的"神兽"，是一种四脚、长尾、头上无角、类似壁虎或蜥蜴的爬虫。

辟邪在汉代以前又称"翼兽"，为中国古代传说中能够除灾的瑞兽，形似狮子而带有双翼。

Chi and Pixie

Chi, is a legendary animal in ancient Chinese myth, with four feet, long tail and without horns, similar to the reptiles like wall gecko and lizard.

Pixie, was also called winged animal before the Han Dynasty. As an auspicious animal who can exorcise evil spirits in ancient Chinese myth, it looks like a lion with two wings.

- 瓷胎仿银螭龙纹圆盖盒（清）
Silver Imitation Porcelain Round Lidded Box with Loong *Chi*'s Pattern (Qing Dynasty, 1616-1911)

- 玉辟邪（魏晋南北朝）
Jade *Pixie* (Wei, Jin Southern and Northern Dynasties, 220-589)

臂搁

　　古时，汉字是由右往左、从上往下书写的。在文字换行时，手腕往往正好触到刚写好、字迹未干的纸上，因此常有手腕、衣袖，以及纸面被弄脏的情况发生，于是便产生了臂搁这种文房用具。臂搁呈微圆筒状，只有两条边与纸接触，因作书写时搁放手臂之用，故称"臂搁"。垫着臂搁书写，不仅能防止墨迹沾上衣袖或弄脏纸面，而且书写者在抄写小字体时感到腕部很舒服，因此，臂搁也称"腕枕"。臂搁还可以充当镇纸压在纸上。

　　臂搁始于唐代，宋代时已经有了关于臂搁的确切记载。明清时的很多古籍都称臂搁为"秘阁"，这是由古代的藏书之所"秘阁"转化而来的。在纸张被发明以前，宫廷

- 铜臂搁（清）
Copper Armrest (Qing Dynasty, 1616-1911)

Armrest

In ancient times, the character was written from the right to the left, from the top to the bottom. While starting a new line, the wrist is usually stained by the newly written characters. So the wrist, sleeve and paper are easily smeared in this situation. In order to avoid such a scenario, the armrest appeared. It is a cylindrical tube and only contacts with the paper through its two edges. As it is used for placing an arm while writing, it is called the armrest. Aside from the function of avoiding the sleeve or paper getting stained, it can make the arm feel comfortable while writing small characters. Therefore, the armrest is also called arm pillow. It is used as paperweight sometimes.

　　Armrest appeared in the Tang Dynasty (618-907). In the Song Dynasty, there was an exact record of it. In the Ming Dynasty and the Qing Dynasty, it was called secret cabinet in many ancient books. The name is transformed from the ancient book storage. Before the invention of paper, the books and secret records stored in palace cabinet were the bamboo slips carved with characters, which were called secret cabinet. After the birth of paper, the secret cabinet wasn't used as

• 象牙臂搁一组（近代）
Ivory Armrest Set (Modern Times)

内的书阁中所藏的图书秘籍都是一些刻写有文字的被称为"秘阁"的竹木简牍。纸张出现后，秘阁不再用作记事存档，而是用来在书写时搁放手臂，再加上"秘阁"与"臂搁"的发音相似，故称"臂搁"。

臂搁的材质很多，有铜、象牙、玉、石、水晶、玻璃、竹、黄杨木、紫檀木、沉香木等。其中尤以竹雕的臂搁最为常见。竹臂搁是将一节竹子一剖两半，上面刻有山水、花鸟、人物及书法的一种臂搁。这些竹臂搁有的古朴而典雅，有的朴素而大方，有的镂雕剔透，显示出不同的艺术效果，深得当时的文人、雅士的喜爱。

log book anymore. They were put under the wrist while writing. Additionally, the pronuncations of the secret cabinet (*Mige*) and armrest (*Bige*) are similar in Chinese, so it is called armrest.

The armrest is made of many materials including copper, ivory, jade, stone, crystal, glass, bamboo, boxwood, rosewood, eaglewood, etc., among which, the bamboo carving armrest is the most common one. It is made of a half bamboo section and carved with landscapes, flowers, birds, figures and inscriptions. These armrests are either plain or elegant. Some are applied with hollow engraving, which have different artistic effects. The armrest was appreciated by the literati at that time.

• 留青花鸟纹竹雕臂搁（清）
Green-retained Bamboo Armrest Carved with Flower and Bird Patterns (Qing Dynasty, 1616-1911)

• 竹刻臂搁（清）
Bamboo Carving Armrest (Qing Dynasty, 1616-1911)

• 留青荷塘纹竹刻臂搁（清）
Green-retained Bamboo Armrest Carved with Lotus Patterns (Qing Dynasty, 1616-1911)

• 竹臂搁（清）
Bamboo Armrest (Qing Dynasty, 1616-1911)

琴棋书画

中国古人把弹奏古琴、下围棋、写书法和绘画合称为"琴棋书画"。这是文人雅士推崇和需要掌握的四种艺术技能，也称"四艺"，用于陶冶情操、修身养性，以显示个人的艺术素养和学识。

"琴"指弹奏古琴。古琴是中国最古老的乐器之一，也是最早的弹拨乐器，至今已有三千多年的历史。古琴历来为文人阶层所重视，被尊为"圣人之器"。

Zither, Chess, Calligraphy and Painting

In ancient China, zither playing, chess playing, calligraphy writing and painting were called "zither, chess, calligraphy and painting". They are four artistic skills upheld by scholars and need to be mastered, also called Four Skills. They can cultivate people's sentiments and indicate their personal artistic attainment and knowledge.

Zither indicates the performance of the seven-stringed zither. The ancient zither is one of the oldest musical instruments in China, and is also the earliest plucked instrument, with at least more than three thousand years of history. It is valued by literati all the time and is honored as the Instrument of Sage.

- 《伯牙鼓琴图》【局部】 王振鹏（元）
  Boya Playing Zither [Part], by Wang Zhenpeng (Yuan Dynasty, 1206-1368)

"棋"指围棋,古称"弈",下围棋则称"对弈"。棋子分黑、白两色。围棋的规则虽简单,但变化无穷,是一种以包围和反包围战术决出胜负的棋艺游戏,从中可以体现出中国古代哲学和文化思想的精髓。

Chess indicates *Weiqi*, also called *Yi* in ancient times. Playing chess is called *Duiyi*. The chess piece has two colors, black and white. The regulation of chess is very simple, however with countless changes. It is a game about surrounding and anti-surrounding. From this game, ancient Chinese philosophy and culture can be reflected.

"书"即书法。书法不仅能给人们带来美的享受,更能陶冶心灵,使心情舒畅。书法是文人综合素养的体现,其学识、品行、胸襟、气质都能在书写的一笔一画中体现出来。

Calligraphy can not only bring the enjoyment of beauty but also cultivate the human mind. It is a reflection of people's comprehensive quality. Their attainment, conduct, tolerance and quality can be seen from every stroke.

● 《芭蕉美人图》 姜隐(明)
图中一女子坐在芭蕉树下,等同伴洗手之后对弈。

Portrait of a Beauty Waiting by the Palm Tree, by Jiang Yin (Ming Dynasty, 1368-1644)
It depicts a lady sitting by the palm tree, waiting for her opponent to come back from washing hands and starting the chess game.

"画"是中国的水墨画。中国的绘画是传统文化的精华,强调"外师造化,中得心源",画的思想内容和艺术表现都会反映出作者的社会认识和审美情趣,体现出作者本人对自然和社会的理解,以及与之关联的道德和修养。

Painting indicates the Chinese ink painting, which is the essence of traditional Chinese culture. It emphasizes that the content and artistic expression of the painting can reflect the author's social consciousness and aesthetic taste. It can reveal his or her consciousness towards nature and society as well as moral accomplishment.

- 书法作品《兰亭序》【局部】 王羲之（晋）
  Preface to Lanting Poem Collection [Part], by Wang Xizhi (Jin Dynasty, 265-420)

- 水墨画《琵琶美人图》 吴伟（明）
  Portrait of a Beauty Holding a Pipa, by Wu Wei (Ming Dynasty, 1368-1644)

> 与砚相关的文房用具

砚滴、水注、水丞

与砚有关的盛水器有三种，一种叫"砚滴"，一种叫"水注"，还有一种叫"水丞"。砚滴、水注和水丞的形状虽然不同，但功用一致，故一般不会同时出现在一个书案上。

砚滴

古人研墨时用此器滴水入砚，故有"砚滴"之称，也叫"水滴"。因为在砚上研墨时所用的水很少，所以砚滴的形体也就小巧玲珑。砚滴大致可分为圆雕动物形和壶形两种，但结构均相同，即器腹中空，可以盛水，都带有进水孔和出水孔。砚滴大约出现在汉代以前。汉代的砚滴古朴而浑厚，与同

> Study Appliances Associated with Inkstone

Water Dropper, Pouring Pot, Water Container

The water storing vessel associated with the inkstone has three kinds. One is called water dropper; one is called pouring pot; another one is called water container. Although they are varied in style, yet with the same function. So they rarely appear on the same table simultaneously.

Water Dropper

While the ancient grinding inkstone, they add water into the inkstone by this tool, which is called water dropper, or slab dropper. As a little water is needed during grinding, the water dropper is made in small size. It has two kinds, the circular engravure animal-designed

• 影青砚滴（北宋）
Green Porcelain Water Dropper (Northern Song Dynasty, 960-1127)

• 龙泉窑舟形砚滴（元）
Boat-shaped Porcelain Water Dropper, from Longquan Kiln (Yuan Dynasty, 1206-1368)

时期的玉兽有异曲同工之妙，多为龟、蛇、熊、羊之形。古籍中关于砚滴的最早记载在汉代的《西京杂记》中："晋灵公墓特大，殉葬品皆朽烂不可识，只有玉蟾蜍一枚，大如拳，腹空容水十合，（广川）王取为砚滴。"魏晋南北朝时期，蛙、龟、蟾蜍等造型的青瓷砚滴较为流行。三国时期的越窑青瓷兔形砚滴外挂绿釉，器形是直立的兔子，前腿捧钵似在饮水，背部带有圆管状的进水孔，构思绝妙。宋元之时，以龙泉窑烧制的砚滴最为奇巧，如舟形砚滴、童子砚滴、鱼形砚滴等。砚滴有陶瓷、金属、玉等各种材质，形制虽然小巧，造型却非常别致，反映出当时的工匠们丰

one and the kettle-designed one. They have the same structure, which is: with a hollowed body where water can be stored, with the inlet and outlet opening. It might appear before the Han Dynasty (206 B.C.-220 A.D.). The one of the Han Dynasty is simple and solemn, and has a lot in common with the jade animal of the same time. It was mostly made in the designs of turtles, snakes, bears and sheep. The earliest record about the water dropper is the *Note of Western Captiul in the Han Dynasty*: the tomb of King Ling of the Jin State is very large. The burial objects are corrupted and cannot be identified. Only a jade toad, with the size of human's fist, can store water in its belly. So the king takes it as his water dropper. In the Wei, Jin, Southern and

• 蟾形铜砚滴（宋）
Toad-shaped Copper Water Dropper
(Song Dynasty, 960-1279)

• 龟形铜砚滴（明）
Turtle-shaped Copper Water Dropper
(Ming Dynasty, 1368-1644)

富的想象力和高超的技艺。

水注

水注也是用以注水于砚的器具，有嘴有把，有的还有盖。古时称壶为"注子"，水注之名本源于此。水注在汉代就已有，多为铜制或瓷制，造型各异。在宋代龙大渊《古玉图谱》的《文房部》一篇中，著录有水注十二式。文震亨的

Northern dynasties (220-589), the green porcelain water droppers with styles of frog, turtle and toad were in prevalence. The green porcelain water dropper of the Three Kingdoms Period (220-280), is covered with a layer of green glaze, with a design of a standing hare: the forelegs holding the bowl and seems like drinking water; while there is a round inlet hole at its back. By the Song Dynasty (960-1279) and the Yuan Dynasty (1206-1368), the most exquisite water dropper had been made from the Longquan Kiln, such as the boat-shaped water dropper, little boy-shaped water dropper, fish-shaped water dropper, etc. They are made of porcelain, metal and jade, with small size yet delicate style, which reflect the rich imagination and skillful craftsmanship of the craftsman at that time.

Pouring Pot

The pouring pot is used to add water into the inkstone, with mouth and handle, sometimes having a lid. The pot was called *Zhuzi* in ancient times, so named *Shuizhu* (pouring pot). It already can be seen in the Han Dynasty, mostly made of copper or porcelain, with various styles. In the *Illustrated Catalog of Ancient Jade* written by Long Dayuan of the

• 青瓷兔形水注（东晋）
Hare-shaped Green Glazed Porcelain Pouring Pot (Eastern Jin Dynasty, 317-420)

• 青釉羊形水注（晋）
Sheep-shaped Green Glazed Porcelain Pouring Pot (Jin Dynasty, 265-420)

• 青釉褐斑鸡首水注（东晋）
Green Glazed and Brown Stained Pouring Pot with Cock Head (Eastern Jin Dynasty, 317-420)

《长物志·器具》载："水注之古铜、玉者俱，有辟邪、蟾蜍、天鸡、天鹿、半身鸬鹚杓、错金雁壶诸式……有铜铸眠牛，以牧童骑牛作注管者最俗，大抵铸为人形即非雅器……陶者有官哥白定，方圆立瓜、卧瓜、双桃、莲房、蒂、茄壶诸式，

Song Dynasty, it lists 12 kinds of pouring pot. In the *Superfluous Things*, by Wen Zhenheng, it records that: the pouring pot is made of copper and jade, with the style of *Pixie*, toad, heavenly rooster, heavenly deer, half cormorant ladle, gold inlaid goose style, and copper sleeping ox style. Use the shepherd boy riding on the ox's back as the outlet opening is the most common one. The pouring pot cast in figures is considered vulgar and of low quality. The porcelain one is mainly fired in Official Kiln, Ge Kiln, Bai Kiln and Ding Kiln, with the style of square or round standing melon, laying melon, double-peach, lotus chamber, flower base leaf, eggplant kettle, etc. The one from Xuan Kiln has polychrome peach pouring pot, pomegranate style, double-melon style and double-mandarin duck style,

• 白玉鸟形尊水注（明）
Bird-shaped White Jade Pouring Pot (Ming Dynasty, 1368-1644)

• 铜蟾形水注（明）
Toad-shaped Copper Pouring Pot (Ming Dynasty, 1368-1644)

宣窑有五采桃注、石榴、双瓜、双鸳诸式……"文中既讲了水注的材质，也讲了水注的造型。宋代还有一种水注，器物的上部有一个气孔，摁住小孔时，水注不滴水，放开后则有水滴下，充分显示了当时工匠的高度智慧和先进的工艺技术。

水丞

水丞为扁圆形、立圆形、瓜棱形及象生形器具，肚大口小，用匙加水，亦名"水盛""水盂""水中丞"等。用砚磨墨时，用小勺从水丞中舀水至砚上。水丞体积不大，但外形美观，放在书案上可作为陈设品。其材质非常丰富，有陶

etc. This book records the texture and style of the pouring pot. In the Song Dynasty, there was a kind of pouring pot, with an air hole on the top. While pressing the hole, the pot will stop dripping; and while releasing the finger, the water will drip out. It absolutely reflects the craftsman's outstanding wisdom and advanced technique of that time.

Water Container

The water container is usually made in oval, round, prismatic or imitation shapes, with a large belly and small mouth, adding water by spoon, also called water filler, water basin, water well, etc. While grinding ink stick by inkstone, people can use a small spoon to add water

• 白釉水丞（宋）
White Glazed Water Container (Song Dynasty, 960-1279)

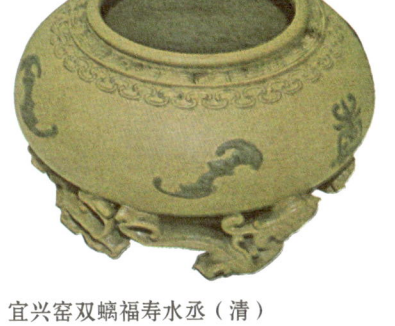

• 宜兴窑双螭福寿水丞（清）
Water Container with the Pattern of Double-loong of the Theme of Good Fortune and Longevity from Yixing Kiln (Qing Dynasty, 1616-1911)

瓷、铜、玉、水晶、绿松石、珊瑚、玛瑙、玻璃、漆、竹、木、珐琅等多种。水丞上的图案更是多种多样，人物、山水、花鸟、虫草、吉祥图案等，应有尽有。

南宋赵希鹄《洞天清禄集》载："古人无水滴，晨起则磨墨，汁盈砚池，以供一日用，墨尽复磨，故有水盂。"西晋时期的水丞是目前见到的最早的实物，当时流行蛙形、蟾形等象生形的青釉水丞，器形优雅而别致，形象生动。唐代流行三彩水丞，色彩艳丽而变化丰富。宋代，影青水丞在文人中受到追捧。影青又称"青白瓷"，釉色白中闪青，青中显白，介于青

from the water container to the inkstone. It is in medium size and with beautiful appearance, which can be placed on table as ornamentation. It can be made of porcelain, copper, jade, crystal, turquoise, coral, agate, glass, lacquer, bamboo, wood, enamel, etc. The patterns painted on the water container are also blazing with color, including the figure, landscape, flower and bird, insect and grass, and other auspicious patterns.

According to the *Collection of Dongtian Qinglu*, by Zhao Xihu in the Southern Song Dynasty (1127-1279), the ancients didn't have the water dropper. They got up early in the morning to grind the ink stick until the ink was full of the whole inkstone which could be used for

• 青釉蟾形水丞（晋）
Toad-shaped Green Glazed Water Container (Jin Dynasty, 265-420)

• 冬青釉堆花云纹水丞（清）
Dongqing Glazed Stacking Flowers Water Container with Could Pattern (Qing Dynasty, 1616-1911)

• 豇豆红釉暗花团龙纹水丞（清）
Cowpea Red Glazed Dark Flower Water Container with Coiled Loong Pattern (Qing Dynasty, 1616-1911)

白之间，犹如青白玉，是江西景德镇窑的独创。到了明代，水丞的样式及材质增多。屠隆在《文具雅编》中记载：此时有琢玉名匠陆子冈用玉做的仿古尊罍水丞，有钧窑烧造的仿古圆肚束口三足水丞，以及各个名窑所烧造的瓮肚圆式、钵盂小口式、菊瓣瓮肚圆足水丞，等

all day. After the ink was used out, they would continue to grind. So the water basin appeared. The water container of the Western Jin Dynasty (265-317) is the earliest one that has been found by people. The frog-style and toad-style green glazed water containers were in prevalence at that time. The vessel shape is elegant and delicate, with a vivid

等。清代的文房用具中，水丞的造型最为丰富多彩，其中又以动物、植物的造型为多，如桃形、海棠形、荷叶形、葫芦形、鹅形、鸭形、海螺形等；口有圆口、菱形口、葵式口、花口等。清朝的《养心殿造办处各作活计清档》中有关于故宫所藏水丞的大量记载，数量之多、品种之全仅次于笔筒。

appearance. By the Tang Dynasty (618-907), the three-color water container had started to prevail. It has gorgeous and changeable glaze colors. In the Song Dynasty, the greenish white porcelain water container was upheld among the literati. Such glaze has a green gloss on the white base or otherwise. The color is between green and white. It looks like the greenish white jade, which was originally created by Jingdezhen Kiln. By the Ming Dynasty (1368-1644), the style and texture of the water container had increased. In the *Compile of Stationery* written by Tu Long, it depicts that: the famous jade carving master, Lu Zigang, produced a water container with the style of ancient *Zun* (a kind of wine vessel used in ancient times). There is three-legged water container with a round

- 青玉桃形雕蝠水丞（明）
  Peach-shaped Greenish White Jade Water Container Carved with Bats (Ming Dynasty, 1368-1044)

- 白玉"瓜瓞绵绵"水丞（明）
  White Jade Water Container Carved with Melon and Butterflies (Ming Dynasty, 1368-1644)

- 青白玉桃形水丞
  Peach-shaped Greenish White Jade Water Container

• 用古玉琮改制的环形水盛（清）
Circular Water Filler Reformed from Ancient Jade *Cong* (Qing Dynasty, 1616-1911)

• 紫晶玉兰花水丞（清）
Magnolia Flower-shaped Amethyst Water Container (Qing Dynasty, 1616-1911)

• 玛瑙荷叶水丞（清）
Lotus Leaf-shaped Natural Agate Water Container (Qing Dynasty, 1616-1911)

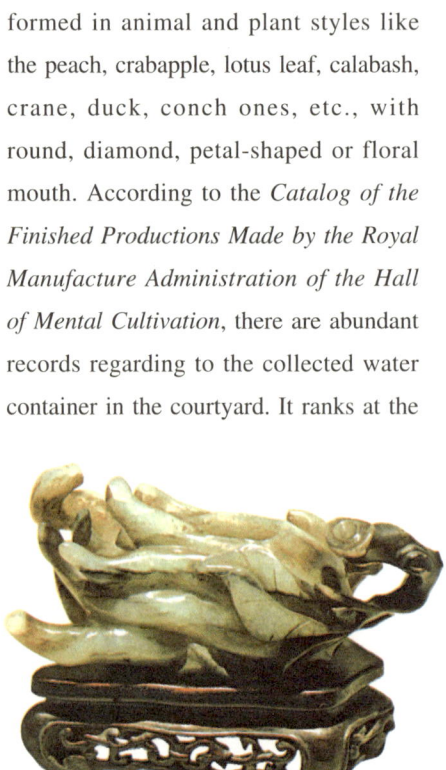

• 青玉佛手水丞（明）
Buddha Palm-shaped Green Jade Water Container (Ming Dynasty, 1368-1644)

belly and small mouth with ancient style fired from Jun Kiln. And other types also prevailed like the bulging belly round water container fired from several famous kilns, the alms bowl style with a small mouth, the bulging belly round foot water container with petal pattern, etc. In the Qing Dynasty (1616-1911), the style of water container was of the richest among other stationery. It is mainly formed in animal and plant styles like the peach, crabapple, lotus leaf, calabash, crane, duck, conch ones, etc., with round, diamond, petal-shaped or floral mouth. According to the *Catalog of the Finished Productions Made by the Royal Manufacture Administration of the Hall of Mental Cultivation*, there are abundant records regarding to the collected water container in the courtyard. It ranks at the

砚屏

砚屏的形状与立在书案上的小插屏相似，被放置在砚端，用于遮障风尘，也被称为"小屏风"。砚屏多以玉、石、陶瓷、漆、竹、木制作，大多被镶嵌在紫檀木或红木的框架中。南宋赵希鹄在《洞天清禄集·砚屏辨》中载："古无砚屏，或铭砚多镌于砚之底与侧，自东坡、山谷始作砚屏，既勒铭于砚，又刻于屏，以表面出之……"从文中可得知，砚屏大约出现在宋代，是由大文学家苏轼和大书法家黄庭坚发明的。明代以后，砚屏的制作工艺愈加精湛，装饰在屏面上的书画、铭文古意盎然，富有诗情画意，带有极其浓厚的书卷气息。

另外，被摆置在砚的前端、山体积不大的奇石制成的砚山也是砚屏的一种。而可被插笔的小屏风叫作"笔屏"。明代屠隆在《文具雅编》中载："笔屏有宋内府制方圆玉花板，用以镶屏插笔最宜。有大理旧石方不盈尺，俨伏山高月小者……皆是天生，初非扭捏。"

second place in quantity and kind right after the brush container.

Inkstone Screen

The inkstone screen is similar to the table screen in shape, which is placed at one end of the inkstone to keep out the wind and dust, also called little screen. It is usually made of jade, stone, porcelain, lacquer, bamboo and wood, and mostly is embedded in the rosewood or redwood's frame. According to the *Collection of Dongtian Qinglu*, by Zhao Xihu in the Southern Song Dynasty, there is no

* 嵌螺钿高士图圆砚屏（清）
Mother-of-pearl Inlaid Round Inkstone Screen with Figure Pattern (Qing Dynasty, 1616-1911)

• 珐琅砚屏
Enamel Inkstone Screen

inkstone screen in ancient times. There were several inscriptions carved on the side or at the bottom of the inkstone. Shu Shi and Huang Tingjian started to produce the inkstone screen. Some were carved either on the inkstone or on the screen. So the inkstone screen appeared in the Song Dynasty, and was invented by Su Shi and Huang Tingjian. After the Ming Dynasty, the craftsmanship of the inkstone screen developed a lot. The calligraphy, painting and inscriptions decorated on the screen are of the ancient style and full of poetic and scholarly ambience.

Besides, the ink mountain produced by peculiar rocks is placed in front of the inkstone. It is also a kind of inkstone screen. And the little screen on which the brush can be stuck in is called brush screen. In the *Compile of Stationery* written by Tu Long, it depicts that: the brush screen has the royal custom made square or round jade flower board, which is very suitable for sticking writing brushes. The marble board with small size is also the natural art of work.

• 嵌青玉镂雕福寿图砚屏（清）
Hollow Engraving Green Jade Board Embedded Inkstone Screen with the Theme of Good Fortune and Longevity (Qing Dynasty, 1616-1911)

屏风

屏风是中国传统家具，具有挡风、遮障及美化环境的功能，同时还是一种精神文化的载体。屏风做工精巧，装饰华丽，或雕刻，或镶嵌。屏风分曲屏和座屏两大类。曲屏又称"围屏""折屏"，是一种可以折叠的多扇屏风，采用攒框做法，扇与扇以合叶相连，扇与扇之间形成一定角度即可竖立摆放在地上。曲屏可以围在床旁用以遮挡，还可以临时摆放，重新划分室内空间。座屏亦称"插屏"，是带有底座、不能折叠的屏风。扇与屏座可装、可卸，分为多扇和独扇，有大有小，大者高3米有余，小者仅20厘米左右。古人常将大座屏作为主要座位后面的屏障，借以显示主人的威严。小插屏常被置于案几之上，多为双面，作陈列、摆设之用，故又称"台屏"。

- 青玉山水图插屏（清）
Green Jade Table Screen Carved with Landscape (Qing Dynasty, 1616-1911)

Screen

The screen is traditional Chinese furniture. Aside from its functions of keeping out the wind, concealing and decorating, it is a cultural carrier. The screen is delicately made with gorgeous decoration. Some are carved with patterns; some are inlaid with decoration items. It has two kinds: folding screen and seat screen. The former is also

- 象牙雕花鸟插屏（清）
Ivory Table Screen Carved with Flowers and Birds (Qing Dynasty, 1616-1911)

called surrounding screen or winding screen. It is a foldable multi-board screen, which is applied with the frame technique. Each board is connected with a hinge. It can stand on the ground while the boards folded at a regular angle. The folding screen can be placed by the bed as a shield, or can be used to rearrange the room space. The seat screen is also called table screen, which is a kind of un-foldable screen with a pedestal. The screen and pedestal can be discharged. It has two styles: multi-board and solo-board. The size is varied from more than 3 m high to 20 cm short. In ancient times, the large seat screen is usually used as the protective screen behind the major seat in order to display the dignity of the master. The little table screen is often placed on table, usually having two sides. It is for display, and ornamentation. So it is also called platform screen.

- "农耕图" 玉插屏（清）

Jade Table Screen Carved with the *Painting of Farming* (Qing Dynasty, 1616-1911)

- 翡翠八仙屏（近代）

Emerald Screen Carved with Eight Immortals (Modern Times)

- 曲屏
Folding Screen

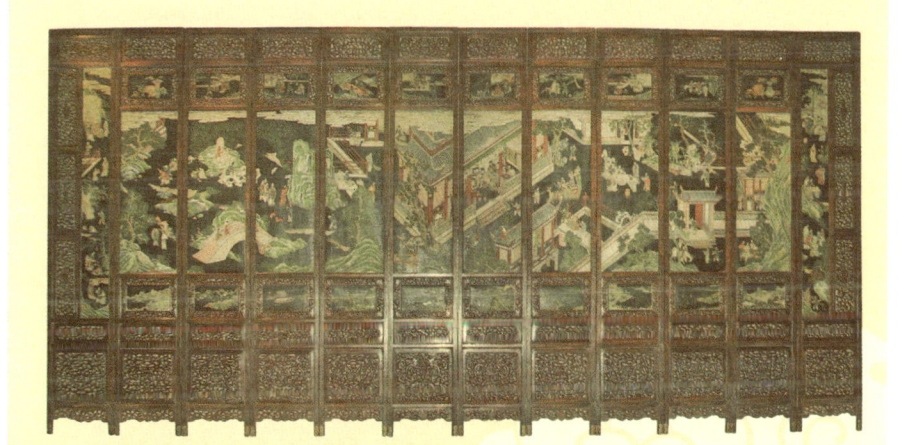

- 黄花梨彩绘人物山水围屏（清）
Scented Rosewood Surrounding Screen Painted with Colored Figures and Landscape (Qing Dynasty, 1616-1911)

> 其他文房用具

印章

　　印章又称"图章",古称"玺"。印章历史悠久,大约在春秋战国时期就已出现,起初只作为商业上买卖货物时的凭证。秦始皇统一中国

> Other Study Appliances

Seal

The seal, is also called stamp, or *Xi* in ancient times. It has a long history and appeared around the Spring and Autumn and Warring periods (770B.C.-221B.C.). In the beginning, it was used as a voucher and letter while exchanging the commodity. After the unification of China by Emperor Shihuang of the Qin Dynasty (221B.C.-206B.C.), the application scope of the seal was extended to the legal certification of personal authority. From

● **秦始皇像**

秦始皇(前259—前210),姓嬴名政,秦朝开国皇帝,也是中国历史上第一位完成统一大业的皇帝。

Portrait of Emperor Shihuang of the Qin Dynasty

Emperor Shihuang of the Qin Dynasty (259 B.C.-210 B.C.), with the surname of Ying, and first name of Zheng, was the founder emperor of the Qin Dynasty and also the first emperor who ever achieved the unification in Chinese history.

"和硕智亲王"金印（清）

"和硕智亲王"金印是清嘉庆皇帝赐给儿子旻宁（后来的道光皇帝）的印章。同时还有一个金册，册封他为和硕智亲王。

Gold Seal Carved with Heshuo Prince of Zhi (Qing Dynasty, 1616-1911)

This gold seal was granted from Emperor Jiaqing to his son Minning (later Emperor Daoguang). There was a gold volume granted to him with the title of Heshuo Prince of Zhi at the same time.

铜质私印（近代）
Copper Private Seal (Modern Times)

后，印章的使用范围扩大，成为证明当权者权益的物品。至汉代，印章开始成为文房清供，为文人所赏玩，后来变成书法、绘画中必不可少的装饰。

印章种类繁多，基本上可分为官印和私印两类。官印即官方所用的印章，由皇家颁发，代表权力。私印是官印以外的印章的统称。有铭刻人的姓名的姓名字号印；有斋馆印，即古人将自己的居室、书斋名字制成印章；有专用于书简

the Han Dynasty (206 B.C.-220 A.D.), the seal started to appear in the study and was appreciated by literati. Later, it became an inevitable decoration in calligraphy and painting.

The seal is varied in kind. Basically, it can be categorized into two kinds: official seal and private seal. The official seal is used by officials and is granted by royal family, representing the authority. While the private seal is the name for the rest seals, which are carved with the name of the owner, or the name of the study, or the letter seal (add greetings in

往来的书简印，即在姓名后再加"启事""言事""再拜""谨封""顿首"等寒暄语印文。此外还有收藏鉴赏印，多用于钤盖书画文物，如收藏类印多被加以"藏书""藏画""珍玩""珍藏"等字样，鉴赏类印多被加以"鉴赏""珍赏""清赏""心赏"等字样，校订类印则多被加以"校订""考定""鉴定""甄定"等字样。

印章的材质为铜、铁、玉、水晶、陶瓷、银、象牙、牛角、木、竹及各种石料。印章的石材产地颇

front of the name like Notice, Speech, Salute Again, Sincerely, and Make a Ceremonious Nod). Additionally, there are collections and appreciation seals used on the works of calligraphy and paintings. The collection is usually carved with Book Collection, Painting Collection, Rare Antique, Precious Collection, etc. And the appreciation one is mostly carved with Appreciation, Precious Work, Pure Appreciation, Extremely Appreciation, etc. The revision seal is mostly carved with Revision, Proofreading, Authentication, Identification, etc.

The seal is mostly made of copper, iron, jade, crystal, porcelain, silver,

- 寿山石人纽方章（清）
  Shoushan Stone Square Seal with Figure Knob (Qing Dynasty, 1616-1911)

- 田黄石松梅纹印章（清）
  Larderite Seal Carved with Pine and Plum Blossoms (Qing Dynasty, 1616-1911)

- 鸡血石印章（清）
  Bloodstone Seal (Qing Dynasty, 1616-1911)

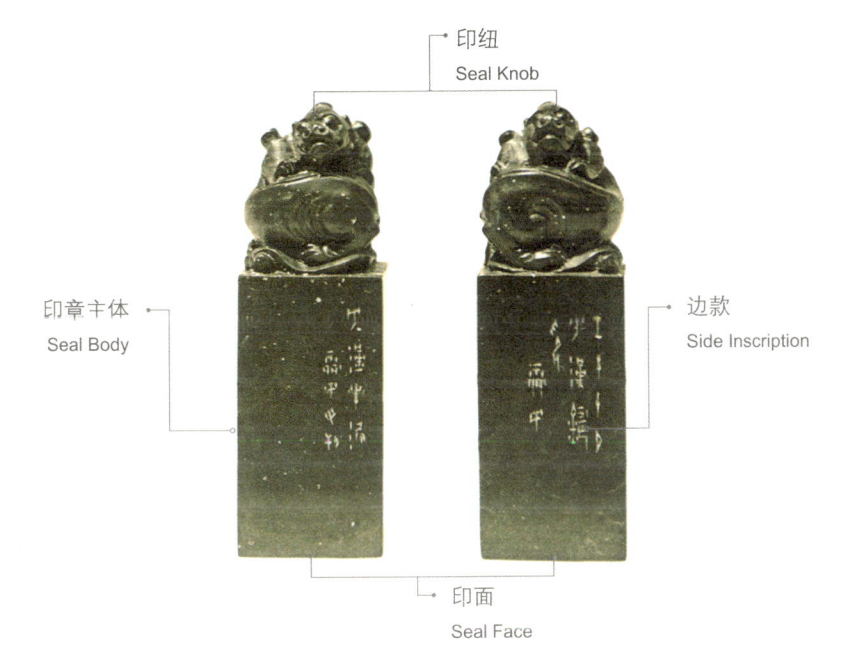

印纽
Seal Knob

印章主体
Seal Body

边款
Side Inscription

印面
Seal Face

- 黑寿山石兽纽方章（清）
  Black *Shoushan* Stone Square Seal with Animal Knob (Qing Dynasty, 1616-1911)

- 阴文雕刻印文"桑妇将蚕养"
  Concave Inscription of "Mulberry Lady Feeding Silkworm"

- 阳文雕刻印文"家在四灵山水间"
  Convex Inscription of "Living in the Mountain along the River"

印章的雕工也是关键。印章的雕刻分为两个方面，一是印文的雕刻，一是印纽的雕刻。常言道，印章的好坏一半在工，一半在料。

The carving technique is a crucial part of the seal production. There are two parts of the seal carving: one is the inscription; the other one is the seal knob. It is said that the quality of a seal depends on the technique and the material equally.

多，仅福建的寿山，以及浙江的青田、昌化三地就有数百种之多。

ivory, xo horn, wood, bamboo and other stones. There are hundreds of stone production areas located in Shoushan, Fujian Province, Qingtian and Changhua,

印纽

印纽是印章上端的雕饰物，不仅具有装饰性，还可系绳于其上，以便于携带。《篆刻学》中载："印之有纽，犹器之有盖，碑之有额，浮屠（佛塔）之有尖，亭榭楼台屋宇之有顶脊鸱甍也。"古代印纽的刻制与封建等级制度密切相关，官印多用印纽来区别官阶。后来，印纽渐渐被强调装饰功能，造型精巧，内容丰富，工艺多样，形成了印纽艺术。

The Seal Knob

The seal knob is the carving ornament on the top of the seal body. Aside from the decorative function, it can be tied with rope for carrying. In the book the *Study of Inscription*, it says that the seal knob as to the seal is like the lid as to the vessel, the headstone as to the tablet, the tented roof as to the pagoda, the ornament on the roof ridge (*Chimeng*) as to the buildings. The carving regulation of the seal knob is closely related to the feudal hierarchy. The knob of the official seal can represent its official ranking. Later, the decorative function of the seal knob gradually took over its identification function. It is with exquisite style and rich content, which makes it a work of art.

- 龙龟纽象牙印（清）
Ivory Seal with Loong and Turtle Knob (Qing Dynasty, 1616-1911)

- 牛纽黄杨木印（明）
Boxwood Seal with an Ox Knob (Ming Dynasty, 1368-1644)

- 鹿纽犀角印（清）
Rhinoceros Horn Seal with Deer Knob (Qing Dynasty, 1616-1911)

八征耄念之宝

　　清代乾隆皇帝的"八征耄念之宝"玺以新疆和田青玉雕制，刻有"八征耄念之宝"六字，交龙纽的刻工也极为精细，显示出了当时精湛的雕刻艺术水平和独特的艺术风格。

　　乾隆在《八征耄念之宝记》一文中说明了镌刻"八征耄念之宝"的原因：七十岁那年，他用唐代诗人杜甫的诗句镌刻了"古稀天子之宝"，勉励自己孜孜不倦，不怠于政事。到了八十大寿时，即将禅位给嘉庆皇帝之前，他又令人刻制了这枚闲章，以《尚书·洪范》的"八征之念"，即仁君、贤帝的八条标准作为"耄耋之念"，时刻谨记在心。同时还以"自强不息"玺作为"八征耄念之宝"玺的副章，与"八征耄念之宝"玺相配使用，进一步表明了他自律、自警的用意。

Treasure of the Eightieth Anniversary

The seal of Treasure of the Eightieth Anniversary made for Emperor Qianlong of the Qing Dynasty (1616-1911) adopted the green jade of Hetian nephrite, carved with *Bazheng Maonian Zhi Bao* (Treasure of the Eightieth Anniversary), six characters. The twisted loong knob was also carved exquisitely, which represents the distinguished carving technique and unique artistic feature at that time.

Emperor Qianlong states the reason for the production of Treasure of the Eightieth Anniversary in the *Article of Treasure of the Eightieth Anniversary*: at his 70 years, he referred to the poem of Du Fu, poet of the Tang Dynasty (618-907) and carved the seal Treasure of the Seventieth Anniversary to encourage himself to work hard. On his 80th birthday, before he was about to abdicate from the throne and passed it to Emperor Jiaqing, he ordered the craftsmen to carve this seal with the meaning of Eight Merits of being a great emperor mentioned in *Shangshu*, in order to keep the regulation in his mind. At the same time, he used the seal of Constantly Strive as its affiliated seal, which can be matched with the seal of Treasure of the Eightieth Anniversary. It reveals his intention of self-discipline and self-warning.

● "八征耄念之宝"玺（清）
Seal of Treasure of the Eightieth Anniversary (Qing Dynasty, 1616-1911)

印泥

　　印泥是中国特有的文房用品，是专供盖印章的颜料。无论是文件签署，还是书法和绘画，都需要使用印章来作钤记。印泥已有两千多年的历史。在纸张没有被发明之前，公私简牍都是写在竹简、木牍上的。封发时，为了防止在传递的过程中泄密，需要用绳将之捆缚，在绳端的交叉处加以封木；然后在封木上加上用湿黏土制成的封泥，再用印章钤上印记，作为封检的标记。纸张出现以后，便改用朱砂加水调成的朱泥，用印章钤于纸上。元代以后，人们开始用油来调和朱砂，这就成为今天的印泥了。

　　印泥主要由朱砂、银砂、艾绒、蓖麻油或茶籽油等调和而成，颜色多为朱红色；其他还有蓝泥、黑泥、茶泥等。还有以红珊瑚、红宝石研成细末调制而成的"八宝印泥"，钤印在纸上可历经数百年仍鲜艳夺目，不会褪色。

Inkpad

The inkpad is an exclusive study appliance in China. It is especially used for storing the pigment of the seal. People will need the inkpad to seal the stamp while signing documents, writing calligraphy or drawing painting. It has a history of more than two thousand years. Before the invention of paper, both the official and private letters were written on the bamboo slips. In order to prevent the leak of the information during the transportation, they should be bound up by rope and added the seal wood at the crossing part of the ropes. Then the seal wood should be covered with the seal mud made of clay. And finally stamp the seal mud with seal as the packing mark. After the birth of paper, people mixed the cinnabar and water to get the red mud which can be stamped on paper by seal. In the Yuan Dynasty (1206-1368), people started to mix oil with the cinnabar, so we get the nowadays inkpad.

　　The main materials of inkpad are cinnabar, silver sand, moxa, castor oil or tea seed oil. The color of the inkpad is mainly red. Some are blue, black and brown. Some will grind the red coral or ruby to a fine powder to make the Eight Treasure Inkpad, which can be stamped on paper with its color indelible through hundreds of years.

- 青花印泥盒
Blue-and-white Inkpad Case

- 印泥
Inkpad

印盒

　　印盒也称印奁、印池、印色盒、印色池，是盛放印泥的文房用具，为书法、绘画必用之物。其材质有多种，如铜、玉、水晶、陶瓷、玻璃、珐琅、象牙、木等。印盒有盖，盒盖与盒身之间有字母口。印盒造型各异，形制多样，有圆形、四方形、长方形、方形委

- 白玉雕螭方印盒（明）

White Jade Square Seal Box Carved with Loong (Ming Dynasty, 1368-1644)

- 白玉圆印盒（清）

White Jade Round Seal Box (Qing Dynasty, 1616-1911)

in Zhejiang Province.

Seal Box

The seal box, also seal case, seal pond, seal pad, or seal pool, is a study appliance used for storing the inkpad, which is an inevitable tool for calligraphy and Chinese painting. It can be made of copper, jade, crystal, porcelain, glass, enamel, ivory, wood, etc. The seal box has a lid. There is a son-and-mother button between the lid and box body. There are various styles and forms including round, quadrate, rectangle, square with crooked corners and oval ones, as well as the multi-level and hollowed out styles. According to the *Kaopan Yushi*, the jade seal box is better than the porcelain one. However, the color is of the best on the porcelain seal box. It is because the porcelain seal box won't leak the oil. The book also depicts that the square seal box fired in the official kiln and Ge Kiln, with eight angles and crooked corners is of the rarest. If there is pattern painted on the exterior of the square seal box from the Ding Kiln, then it can be seen as the best one. As early as the Song Dynasty (960-1127), almost every famous kiln had once fired the seal box. It has many

角、椭圆、多层多屉、镂空等。《考槃余事》载:"诸玩器玉当较胜于瓷,唯印色池以瓷为佳,而玉亦未能胜也。"这是因为瓷做的印盒绝不会渗漏印油。《考槃余事》又载:"印色池,官哥窑方者,尚有八角、委角者最难得。定窑方池外有印花纹甚佳,此亦少者。"早在宋代,各个名窑就烧造过瓷印盒。瓷印盒的品种有青花、五彩、斗彩、粉彩、颜色釉等。印盒的出现不会晚于唐。在清代的宫廷中,印盒主要有两类:一类为钤小形玺印所用;另一类是政务钤盖宝玺所用的巨型印盒,直径约有50厘米,是以锡制成的圆盒,其中盛满印泥。

kinds including the blue-and-white, polychrome, clashing color, famille rose and colored glazed ones, etc. The appearance of the seal box is no later than the Tang Dynasty. In the Qing Dynasty, there were two kinds of seal box in the palace: one was used for storing the small seal; the other was used for storing the huge official seal, with a diameter of

- 青花龙凤大印盒(清)
Large Blue-and-white Seal Box Painted with Loong and Phoenix (Qing Dynasty, 1616-1911)

- 景德镇窑粉彩描金八吉祥纹印盒(清)
Gold-traced Famille Rose Seal Box Painted with Eight Auspicious Patterns from Jingdezhen Kiln (Qing Dynasty, 1616-1911)

- 青花釉里红寿山福海印盒(清)
Blue-and-white Underglazed Red Seal Box with the Theme of Longevity Mountain and Auspicious Ocean (Qing Dynasty, 1616-1911)

帖架

帖架是临习书法字帖或临摹中国画必不可少的用具，是一台直立、固定的架子，可支展和折合，既灵活，又便捷。帖架的材质多为竹、木或金属，有些帖架的底部还设有小抽屉，可放置笔、墨等小物品。明、清两代的文人使用的帖架多以紫檀、黄花梨等名贵木料制成，形制或简约，或繁复，设计和制作都十分精巧。清末学者叶昌炽在《语石》中记录道："读碑，铺儿平视，不如悬之壁间，能得其气脉神理。于是临池家制为帖架，对面传神，如灯取影。" 用帖架可以使书写或作画的人以直视的角度进行临摹，看一笔画一笔，看一字写一字，不但省力，还可以仔细观察所临字帖和绘画的用笔、用墨、用色及构图，体会范本的神韵。

50 centimeters, made of tin, shaped in a round style and filled with inkpad.

Copybook Holder

The copybook holder is an inevitable tool while imitating the copybook and learning calligraphy. It is a vertical foldable standing rack, which is flexible and convenient. It is mostly made of bamboo or metal. Some will set a little drawer at the bottom in which the brush and inkstone can be placed. In the Ming Dynasty and the Qing Dynasty, the most of literati used the copybook holder, which is mainly made of precious wood material like rosewood and scented rosewood, with either a simple or complicated structure. All is delicately designed. According to the *Talk about Stone*, by Ye Changchi in the late Qing Dynasty, it depicts that reading the tablet, and looking at the front horizontally is no better than hanging with arms. It can make the reader comfortable physically. So I had it made into copybook holder

- 折叠式红木帖架（清）
Foldable Redwood Copybook Holder (Qing Dynasty, 1616-1911)

山子

在清代文房的儿案上，山子是常见的陈设品，也具有镇纸和笔架的作用。山子有玉、翡翠、青金石、玛瑙、玻璃、陶瓷等不同材for reading. The copybook holder can allow the reader to practice and imitate the copybook with a straight angle. It not only helps save the strength, but also let the reader carefully observe the copybook or the strokes, ink shade, color choosing and the composition of the painting.

Rockwork *(Shanzi)*

In the study of the Qing Dynasty, the rockwork is a common display on the table. It also can be used as paperweight and brush rack. The rockwork is mostly made of jade, emerald, lapis lazuli, agate, glass and porcelain. The theme and shape are varied, and generally have an auspicious meaning.

- 玉山子（清）
  Jade Rockwork (Qing Dynasty, 1616-1911)

- 青金石雕山水御题诗山子（清）
  Lapis Lazuli Rockwork Carved with Landscape and Inscription (Qing Dynasty, 1616-1911)

质，题材和形状也多种多样，多有吉祥之寓意。

另外，文房清供中也包括自然形态的石质山子，如大理石、菊花石、孔雀石、英石、灵璧石等。

文房套具

文房套具指将小件的笔、墨、纸、砚这文房四宝同与之相关的文具集中起来，用特定的箱匣盛装，专供人外出时在旅途中书写，故明代人称之为"途利"。因收贮文房器具的品类和数量不同，所用箱匣的种类、大小也不尽相同，有些器具还可被盛放于盘子中。明末出现的"官皮箱"实际上就是官员或文人出门时携带的文具箱。有的文具箱设计巧妙，打开可成小桌。清代制作的文具箱匣，不仅装在其内的文具工艺精湛、器形新颖，而且不少箱匣本身就雕刻精细、制作工整，有螺钿镶嵌、雕漆、竹刻等。特别是明清时期宫廷内使用的文具箱，充分反映出明、清两代工艺制作的水平和特点，将古代文房用具的艺术性推向极致。如有的文具箱

• 微雕诗文象牙笔、青玉山子（清）
Ivory Writing Brush Carved with Inscription, Green Jade Rockwork (Qing Dynasty, 1616-1911)

Besides, there is the natural rockwork among the study appliances, like the marble, chrysanthemum stone, malachite, *Ying* Stone, *Lingbi* Stone, etc. Some are equipped with a rosewood pedestal.

Set Appliance

The set appliance indicates the case in which the small sized Four Treasures of the Study, writing brush, ink stick, paper and inkstone can be put together. It is used for outdoor writing and painting. So it was called Way Benefit in the Ming Dynasty (1368-1644). As the type and

• 紫漆描金文具匣（清）
Gold-traced Purple Lacquer Stationery Case (Qing Dynasty, 1616-1911)

匣内除了文房用具，还有书法小卷、对数表、金属刀具、壁瓶、古玩等物，而且大多以名贵的玉石、玛瑙、水晶琢制，还有的以蜜蜡、金星玻璃等稀有材质制成。乾隆皇帝曾亲题《四藏书屋咏文房四事（有序）》，记叙了紫漆描金团花纹四事文具匣的制作经过。

quantity it stored are varied, the case has different sizes. Some appliance can be placed in dish. In the late Ming Dynasty, the official leather case appeared. It is actually the suitcase carried by the officials or literati. Some of them are designed exquisitely, which can be assembled into a small table. The case made in the Qing Dynasty is not only decorated carefully but also has many creative tools. Many cases are produced with delicate carving and inlaid with pearl and carved lacquer, bamboo carving, etc. Especially the suitcase used in the courtyard in the Ming Dynasty and the Qing Dynasty, fully reflects the craftsmanship and features at that time, which has lifted the aesthetic standard of the study appliance to a brand new level. For example, aside from the stationery, some cases even contain the small scrolls of calligraphy, the log tables, metal knives, jade vases and other antiques, most of which are made from precious jade, agate, crystal, beeswax and gold star glass. Emperor Qianlong once wrote the inscription for the *Four Things of the Study*, in which the book depicts the production procedure of the gold-traced purple lacquer four-thing stationery case painted with coiled flower pattern.

文房清供的材质及制作工艺
Materials and Craftsmanship of Stationery and Bibelot in Ancient Studies

　　文房清供材质丰富，用途广泛，所用材料包括玉、石、金属、漆、陶瓷、玻璃、珐琅、竹、木、象牙、角、匏等；制作工艺也非常繁复，涵盖了铸造、雕刻、琢制等加工工艺。

Stationery and bibelot in ancient studies are produced from various materials and have a broad application scope. Many materials are applied in the production, including jade, stone, metal, lacquer, porcelain, glass, enamel, bamboo, wood, ivory, horn, calabash, etc. And the craftsmanship is also complicated which involves many processing techniques like foundry, sculpture, carving, etc.

> 金属

很多文房用具是以金属制作的，如铜、银、铁、锡等，有些还表现为在铜中掺入金、银、铅，制成各种合金。最早的金属文具出现于商代，是专用于修治简牍的青铜书刀。而历代常见的金属文具多是以铜制作的注水器，如水丞、水注、砚滴等，这主要是因为铜有不

> Metal

Many study appliances are made of metal, such as copper, silver, iron, tin, etc. Some are made of various alloys by mixing gold, silver and lead into copper. The earliest metal stationery, which appeared in the Shang Dynasty (1600 B.C.-1046 B.C.), were bronze knives specially used to trim bamboo and wooden slips (materials for ancient books). However, the commonly seen metal stationery in many dynasties is copper water fillers, such as water containers, pouring pots, water droppers, etc. The reason for using copper is that copper does not rust

• 铜童戏水丞（清）
Copper Water Container with a Design of a Child Playing around It (Qing Dynasty, 1616-1911)

腐于水的优点。除此之外，还有铜制的笔架、墨盒、臂搁、镇纸等。

金属文具上有金银错、镏金、刻线、烧蓝、景泰蓝等装饰工艺。

錾刻

錾刻是用凿子或极锋利的刀在铸好的金属器上刻划纹饰、图案和文字。线条要十分纤细，运线要流畅。

金银错

"错"就是预先在铁器或铜器上錾凿出精细的纹饰线条，在其上镶金银丝或金银片，再进行打磨，使器物表面平滑，达到严丝合缝的效果。用这种方法还可以错铜、错石、错漆。

in water. In addition, there are copper writing brush racks, ink boxes, armrests, paperweights, etc.

Metal stationery has the decorative craftsmanship of inlaid gold and silver, gilding, engraving lines, bluing, cloisonné, etc.

Engraving with Chisel

This method is to engrave or draw ornamentation, patterns and words with a chisel or a very sharp knife. The lines should be very slender, and the process of engraving should be smooth.

Inlaid Gold and Silver

Inlaying is to engrave elaborate decoration lines on iron or bronze ware before embedding gold and silver purl or pieces and then polish to make the surface smooth and seamless. Copper, stones and lacquer can also be inlaid in this way.

- 铜错银羊形镇纸（清）
Sheep-shaped Copper Paperweight Inlaid with Silver (Qing Dynasty, 1616-1911)

镏金

镏金即将金和水银合成的金汞剂涂在铜器表面，然后加热，使水银蒸发，金就附着在铜器表面，而不会脱落。

珐琅

珐琅工艺有多种分类。其中，铜胎掐丝珐琅是在铜胎上掐丝、点蓝后经高温烧制而成的。因它盛行于明代景泰年间，并以蓝色为主调，故名"景泰蓝"。錾胎珐琅表现为在金属胎体上雕錾，使纹样的轮廓线突起，在其下陷处填充珐琅料，经焙烧、磨光、镀金而成。铜胎画珐琅即先在铜胎上敷一层白釉，焙烧后填彩釉，再焙烧、镀金、磨光。还有一种烧蓝工艺，即在银胎的器物上以低温珐琅釉焙烧，釉色比铜胎珐琅乌暗。

Gilding

Gilding is to apply the gold mercurial which is a synthesis of gold and mercury to the surface of bronze ware and then heat it to evaporate mercury. In this way, gold will be left on the surface of bronze ware and will not fall off.

Enamel

As one kind of Enamel techniques, gilt-bronze and cloisonné enamel refers to filigree and blue enamel on the copper body fired at high temperature. Since it prevailed in the Jingtai Period, Ming Dynasty (1450-1456), and had the main color of blue, hence the name *Jingtailan* (cloisonné, *Lan* means blue). Engraved enamel means engraving on metal body to make the outline of patterns protruding, fill enamel glaze in the sag of the outline, then fire, polish, gild it and finally make it. Painting enamel on copper body is to deposit a layer of white glaze on the

- 珐琅镇纸（清）
Enamel Paperweight (Qing Dynasty, 1616-1911)

copper body at first, fire it and then fill the glaze. It is made after firing, gilding and polishing. Another technique is the bluing process, which is to fire the glaze on silver ware under low-temperature. The glaze made in this way is darker than enamel glaze on copper ware.

- 嵌珐琅双龙戏珠圆笔洗（清）
Round Enamel Brush Washer with the Pattern of Two Loongs Playing with a Ball (Qing Dynasty, 1616-1911)

- 珐琅笔山
Mountain-shaped Enamel Writing Brush Rack

- 珐琅水丞
Enamel Water Container

> 陶瓷

陶瓷是陶器和瓷器的总称。陶器以黏土为原料，成形后经800摄氏度至1000摄氏度的高温烧成。瓷器以瓷土为原料，经1200摄氏度至1300摄氏度的高温烧制而成。

汉代以后，出现了由青釉、青黄釉等单色釉制成的文房用具，如水注、水丞、砚滴、笔筒等。

唐代的陶瓷文具除了有白釉、黄绿釉、酱褐釉等单色釉外，还出现了黄釉绿彩、黄釉褐彩、褐釉黄绿彩等釉下彩。尤以唐三彩最为独特，唐代初期盛行三彩釉的陶制文具。虽说是"三彩"，其实并不限于在一件器物上只用三种色釉，而是在白色的陶胎上涂以黄、赭、绿、蓝、紫等多种色釉。三彩的釉色比单色釉更加鲜艳夺目、绚丽多

> Ceramics

The ceramic is a general term for pottery and porcelain. With the main raw material of clay, pottery is made by being fired at a temperature of 800-1000 degrees Celsius after being formed. Porcelain, with the raw material of china clay, is made after being fired at a temperature of 1,200-1,300 degrees Celsius.

After the Han Dynasty (206 B.C.-220 A.D.), the celadon, greenish yellow glazed and other monochrome glazed tools in ancient Chinese studies appeared, such as pouring pots, water container, water droppers, brush containers, etc.

In the Tang Dynasty (618-907), besides white, yellowish green, brown or other monochrome glazes, underglaze colors like yellow glaze with green or brown patterns or brown glaze with yellow or green patterns also appeared. The most unique glaze in the Tang

三彩釉带盖水盂（唐）
Three-color Glazed Water Basin with Lid
(Tang Dynasty, 618-907)

彩。此时，北方著名的白瓷窑场邢窑、南方瓷器烧造水平最高的青瓷窑场越窑，以及寿州窑、长沙窑也烧制了大量的瓷文房用具。

Dynasty was the tri-color glaze and the tricolored pottery stationery prevailed in the early Tang Dynasty. Although it was called "tri-color", in fact, the colors are not limited to only three. It is to glaze yellow, reddish blue, green, blue, purple or many other colors on white pottery. Tri-colored glaze is brighter and more colorful than monochrome glaze. In the Tang Dynasty, the famous white porcelain kiln Xing Kiln, the celadon porcelain kiln Yue Kiln which represented the highest level of firing and Shouzhou Kiln and Changsha Kiln all produced much porcelain stationery.

In the Song Dynasty (960-1279), many famous kilns, such as Ding Kiln,

唐代的名窑

邢窑是唐代最著名的白瓷窑场，窑址在今河北内丘，当时属邢州，故名。邢窑的白瓷胎质细腻，色纯白而极坚硬，风格朴素。

越窑是晋代、唐代最为著名的青瓷窑场，中心窑址在浙江余姚一带，唐代时属越州，故名。自东汉时起，越窑就是中国瓷器生产的主要窑场；五代时曾设官监造越窑青瓷，专供宫廷使用；北宋后，越窑逐渐衰落。越窑青瓷胎质坚硬，釉色纯净

邢窑白釉"盈"字款盒（唐）
White Glazed Box with Chinese Character *Ying* from Xing Kiln
(Tang Dynasty, 618-907)

如翠，纹饰多为刻花和印花，纹样活泼而优美。

寿州窑为唐代瓷窑，窑址在今安徽淮南，唐代属寿州，故名。唐代以前烧制青瓷，唐代以后改烧黄釉瓷，胎体厚重，釉面光润。该窑曾烧制过一些水注等文具。

长沙窑为唐代名窑，在今湖南长沙铜官镇，亦称"铜官窑"。所烧制器物的釉色有青、黄、白、黑等。首创釉下彩器和在瓷器上进行彩绘的装饰技法，即在青釉下用褐色或绿色的斑点组成图案，或用笔在白釉或青黄釉下描绘图案。

Famous Kilns in the Tang Dynasty (618-917)

Xing Kiln, the most famous kiln in the Tang Dynasty (618-917) is located in Neiqiu County, Hebei Province. It was within Xingzhou in the Tang Dynasty, hence the name. The white porcelain of Xing Kiln was delicate, pure white and hard with a simple style.

Yue Kiln was the most famous porcelain kiln in the Jin Dynasty (265-420) and the Tang Dynasty. Its center was in the vicinity of Yuyao, Zhejiang Province and belonged to Yuezhou in the Tang Dynasty, hence the name. Since the Eastern Han Dynasty (25-220), Yue Kiln started to be the main kiln for producing Chinese porcelain. During the Five dynasties (907-960), the government appointed officials to supervise Yue Kiln which produced celadon glaze specifically for court use; after the Northern Song Dynasty, Yue Kiln gradually declined. Celadon glaze of Yue Kiln is hard with pure glaze like emerald, its decorations are engraved and printed flowers with lively and beautiful patterns.

• 越窑青釉四足水丞（唐）
Green Glazed Quadruped Water Container, from Yue Kiln (Tang Dynasty, 618-907)

Shouzhou Kiln, the porcelain kiln in the Tang Dynasty is located in Huainan, Anhui Province. It belonged to Shouzhou in the Tang Dynasty, hence the name. It produced green glaze before the Tang Dynasty and changed to yellow glazed porcelain after the Tang Dynasty. The Shouzhou glaze is heavy with a smooth glazed surface. Some pouring pots were made in Shouzhou Kiln.

Changsha Kiln, the famous kiln in the Tang Dynasty, is now located in Tongguan town, Changsha, Hunan Province and is also known as Tongguan Kiln. Items fired here had blue, yellow, white, black glaze, and so on. It first made the underglaze ware and developed the techniques to paint colorful decorative patterns on porcelain, namely painting brown or green spot patterns under celadon glaze, or drawing patterns on the white or greenish yellow glaze.

宋代时，很多著名的窑场，如定窑、龙泉窑、汝窑、钧窑等都生产有大量的陶瓷文具，如水丞、水注、砚滴、笔洗、香炉等。江西景德镇窑生产的青白瓷文具光洁而精美，釉色白中闪青，青中显白，介于青白之间，犹如青白玉。这种青白瓷也被称为"影青瓷"。如当时常见的影青瓜棱形水注、水丞，形态似瓜，腹壁刻有瓜棱纹，瓜棱之间的釉色有深浅之别，但过渡自然，而且胎质坚硬而细腻，器型独特而纤巧。除此之外，陕西耀州窑的青瓷文具、福建德化窑的白瓷文具胎、釉浑然一体，光润如玉，都非常精美。

- 景德镇窑青白釉印花缠枝莲荷纹笔插（宋）
Greenish White Glazed Brush Container with Pattern of Intertwined Branches and Lotus, from Jingdezhen Kiln (Song Dynasty, 960-1279)

Longquan Kiln, Ru Kiln, Jun Kiln, etc., all produced large amounts of porcelain stationery, such as water containers, pouring pots, water droppers, brush washers, incense burners, etc. Blue-and-white porcelain stationery made in Jingdezhen Kiln, Jiangxi Province has a beautiful luster and its glaze is white flashing green, green reflecting white. The color is between green and white, like green jade. This blue-and-white porcelain is also known as "shadow celadon". The commonly seen shadow celadon pouring pots and water containers have the shape of melon and the prismatic patterns on their belly. The glaze between prismatic patterns is different in depth, but with a natural transition. The glaze is hard and delicate, with unique and slim shape. In addition, celadon stationery of Yaozhou Kiln in Shaanxi Province and white porcelain stationery in Dehua Kiln in Fujian Province all have integrated and smooth shapes and glaze like jade, which are delicate and beautiful.

It is said that the blue-and-white porcelain which was first made in the Song Dynasty and mature in the Yuan Dynasty (1206-1368), reached its zenith in the Ming Dynasty (1368-1644) and the Qing Dynasty (1616-1911). Blue-

宋代五大名窑

定窑的窑址在河北曲阳县一带，古属定州，故名。定窑从唐代开始生产白瓷，至宋代而著名。定窑以烧造白色素瓷为主，胎薄而坚致，色白而略带微黄；釉色为米色，施釉极薄，可见胎。定窑瓷装饰技法精巧，以印花、划花和堆花为主，秀丽而典雅，别具一格。

龙泉窑的窑址在浙江龙泉县，故名。龙泉窑的特点是胎薄如纸，釉色以翠青、梅子青和粉青为最佳，釉色柔和似玉。

汝窑的窑址在古称"汝州"的河南临汝县，故名。汝窑所产瓷器胎土细润，釉色近似雨过天晴的颜色，以淡青色为主。装饰技法以釉下印花为主，图案多为花鸟，布局严谨，构图完美。

钧窑在今河南禹县，唐宋时为钧州辖地，故名。钧窑瓷以烧制色釉"窑变"为特色，故有"千钧万变，意境无穷"一说。基本釉色表现为通体天青色与紫红斑相间，色彩错综复杂，绚丽多彩。

官窑也称"两宋官窑"。据传，北宋时在汴京（今河南开封）一带设立窑场，南宋时在浙江杭州附近设立窑场。官窑烧造的青瓷胎薄，呈灰、黑、褐三色；釉厚，晶莹、润泽，如美玉，釉面多有开片；器口至底部露胎处呈灰色或铁色，有"紫口铁足"之称。

Five Famous Kilns in the Song Dynasty

Ding Kiln is located in the Quyang County, Hebei Province and belongs to Dingzhou in ancient times, hence the name. Ding Kiln produced white porcelain in the Tang Dynasty and became famous in the Song Dynasty. Ding Kiln mainly makes hard white porcelain with the slightly yellowish color; the cream colored glaze is thin and the pottery is visible. With sophisticated decorative techniques, Ding Kiln focuses on the printing, scratching and stacking of flowers, which are beautiful, elegant and unique.

Longquan Kiln is located in Longquan County, Zhejiang Province, hence the name.

• 龙泉窑青釉贴花双鱼纹笔洗（元）
Appliqué Green Glazed Bursh Washer with Pattern of Double Fish, from Longquan Kiln (Yuan Dynasty, 1206-1368)

It is characterized by the thin base like a piece of paper and the emerald, plum and pinkish green glaze which has the mild color of jade.

Ru Kiln is located in Linru County, Henan Province which was named Ruzhou in the ancient time, hence the name. Ru Kiln produces porcelain with fine and glossy soil and the glaze is light green, like the color of the sky after rain. The main decorative technique is underglaze printing and the patterns are mainly flowers and birds under the rigorous layout and perfect composition.

Jun Kiln is located in Yuxian County, Henan Province today and belonged to Junzhou in the Tang Dynasty and the Song Dynasty, hence the name. Jun Kiln porcelain is famous for firing colorful fambe glaze (means changes after firing in the kiln), so people call it "wonderful changes with infinite artistic conception". The basic glaze is toned in azure with purplish red spots, which are bright and colorful.

Guan Kiln is also known as the official kiln in the Northern Song Dynasty (960-1127) and the Southern Song Dynasty (1127-1279). It is said that kilns were set up in the vicinity of Bianjing (now Kaifeng, Henan Province) in the Northern Song Dynasty and in the vicinity of Hangzhou, Zhejiang Province in the Southern Song Dynasty. The celadon porcelain made in official kilns is thin with the color of gray, black and brown; it has a thick glaze glistening like jade and there are cracked glazes on the surface; at the mouth and the bottom of the ware where bases are exposed, the colors are gray or like iron, so it is called "purple mouth and iron feet".

- 汝窑笔洗（北宋）
Brush Washer from Ru Kiln (Northern Song Dynasty, 960-1127)

- 钧窑玫瑰红釉鼓式笔洗（北宋）
Drum-shaped Rose-red Glazed Brush Washer from Jun Kiln (Northern Song Dynasty, 960-1127)

相传创始于宋代、成熟于元代的青花瓷，在明、清两代达到鼎盛。青花是釉下彩的一种，即先用钴料在瓷坯上描绘纹饰，再上透明釉，经1200摄氏度以上的高温还原焰烧成，纹饰清澈而典雅，永不褪色。青花文具种类繁多，有笔架、

- 景德镇窑青花五彩莲花龙纹镂空盖盒（明）
Blue-and-white Lidded Box with Lotus and Polychrome Loong Patterns from Jingdezhen Kiln (Ming Dynasty, 1368-1644)

- 青花包袱纹调色盘（明）
Blue-and-white Palette with Cloth-wrappers Pattern (Ming Dynasty, 1368-1644)

and-white is one of underglaze colors. The production process is: drawing decorations on the porcelain bases with cobalt, glazing it the transparent color and firing it by the reducing flame at a temperature above 1,200 degrees Celsius. In this way, the patterns are clear and elegant and will never fade. There are many kinds of blue-and-white stationery, such as brush racks, brush containers, armrests, ink boxes, paperweights, various water fillers, etc. The polychrome porcelain stationery which was called "five colors in the blue-and-white porcelain" in the Ming Dynasty's literature is the famous stationery and bibelot in ancient studies. Since overglazing blue technique had not been invented at that time, the underglazing blue-and-white technique were used to present the blue color. By adding the red, yellow, green, black, etc., as overglazed paints, the famous polychrome porcelain was made. The enamel and famille rose stationery made by the Qing court has rich patterns, bright colors, and presents the magnificent and imperial dignity. The enamel is a new kind of method that absorbs the practices of Western porcelain paintings and belongs to the low temperature overglazed color. It has

笔筒、臂搁、印盒、镇纸、各类注水器等。明代文献中名为"青花间装五彩"的五彩瓷文房用具更成为文房清供中的名品。由于当时釉上蓝彩还未被发明，用釉下青花来表现蓝彩，再配以釉上的红、黄、绿、黑等彩料，就成为著名的五彩瓷。清代宫廷所制的珐琅彩、粉彩文房用具图案丰富，颜色明艳，富丽堂皇，尽显皇家气派。珐琅彩是借鉴西洋瓷画珐琅的做法创烧出来的新品种，属于低温釉上彩的一种，胎壁极薄，釉色多种，色彩娇艳，层次分明，立体感强。粉彩瓷则是在五彩瓷的基础上创烧出来的新品种，纹饰艳丽，技艺精湛，具有极高的艺术价值。

• 青花缠枝莲纹笔洗（明）
Blue-and-white Brush Washer with Intertwined Flower Branches Patterns (Ming Dynasty, 1368-1644)

• 青花鱼藻纹葵瓣笔洗（现代）
Blue-and-white Sunflower-pedal-shaped Brush Washer with Fish and Algae Patterns (Modern Times)

• 青花描金粉彩山水人物纹笔床（清）
Blue-and-white Gold-traced Brush Rest with Landscape and Human Figure Patterns (Qing Dynasty, 1616-1911)

a thin glaze and various colors, which is clearly structured and dimensional. Famille rose porcelain is a new kind based on the polychrome porcelain. Made of high skills, it has bright decorations and high artistic value.

　　Stationery made of purple clay also flourished in the Ming Dynasty

景德镇窑

江西景德镇窑是元代以来中国最大的窑场。宋代时就创烧了著名的青白瓷（影青）；元代的著名制品表现为青花、釉里红和卵白釉几种形式；明代时成为中国的制瓷中心，创造出丰富多彩的各种色釉和彩饰，如甜白、霁红、霁青、青花五彩等；清代在明代的基础上，品种更是不断创新，新创了釉上彩、粉彩、珐琅彩等。

Jingdezhen Kiln

Jingdezhen Kiln in Jiangxi Province was the largest kiln after the Yuan Dynasty. It made the famous bluish white porcelain (shadow blue) in as early as the Song Dynasty; In the Yuan

- 景德镇窑黄釉人物纹笔筒（清）
Yellow Glazed Brush Container with Figure Pattern from Jingdezhen Kiln (Qing Dynasty, 1616-1911)

- 景德镇窑粉彩石纹笔筒（清）
Famille Rose Gold-traced Brush Container with Framed Stone Patterns from Jingdezhen Kiln (Qing Dynasty, 1616-1911)

- 景德镇窑粉彩人物纹笔筒（清）
Famille Rose Brush Container Painted with Human Figure from Jingdezhen Kiln (Qing Dynasty, 1616-1911)

- 景德镇窑墨彩山水纹笔筒（清）
Brush Container with Ink-colored Landscape Pattern from Jingdezhen Kiln (Qing Dynasty, 1616-1911)

Dynasty, it produced the famous blue-and-white, underglaze red and egg white glaze; In the Ming Dynasty, it became the center for producing porcelain and created a colorful variety of glazes and polychrome porcelain decorations, such as sweet white, shiny red, sky-clearing blue, blue-and-white and so on; on the basis of the Ming Dynasty, kinds were innovated and the overglaze colors, famille rose, enamel were created in the Qing Dynasty.

• 景德镇窑五彩梅花笔洗（明）
Polychrome Brush Washer with Plum Blossom Patterns from Jingdezhen Kiln (Ming Dynasty, 1368-1644)

• 景德镇窑青花红彩御制诗水丞（清）
Blue-and-white Red-colored Imperial Water Container Painted with Poem Written by Emperor from Jingdezhen Kiln (Qing Dynasty, 1616-1911)

• 景德镇窑豇豆红釉水丞（清）
Cowpea Red Glazed Water Container from Jingdezhen Kiln (Qing Dynasty, 1616-1911)

紫砂文具在明、清两代达到兴盛。紫砂器产于江苏宜兴，是用被称为"陶中陶"的紫砂泥烧制而成

- 紫砂描金彩绘山水人物纹大笔筒（清）
Gold-traced Brush Container with the Colored Design of Landscape and Human Figure from Yixing Kiln (Qing Dynasty, 1616-1911)

- 紫砂干果笔洗（清）
Purple Clay Brush Washer with the Design of Dried Fruit (Qing Dynasty, 1616-1911)

and the Qing Dynasty. Purple clay ware, first produced in Yixing, Jiangsu Province, was pottery ware fired out of purple clay which was called Best of Pottery. Different from other glazed pottery productions, purple clay ware has its own colors, such as the colors of chestnut, liver, purple bronze, pear-skin, sky-blue, dark green, and so on. It also has good air permeability and a subtle gloss on its surface. The longer it is used, the more lustrous surface like jade ware it will form. So such a characteristic is called cultivatable. So purple clay stationery enjoys an equal reputation with purple clay teapots and is loved by many scholars. In addition to water fillers, some brush racks, brush containers, armrests, etc. are also made of purple clay. The famous pottery maker Chen Zhiyuan in the Kangxi and Yongzheng periods (1662-1735) of the Qing Dynasty, was adept at making various purple clay study tools. The fruit-shaped stationery made by him was sophisticated, exquisite and had its own features. Such as bamboo-shaped purple clay water container is like a lying bamboo shoot and the dense ribs and fibers, the traces left by insects' bites are all portrayed vividly. It is the same

的陶器。以紫砂制成的器物与上了釉的陶制品不同，本身就呈栗色、猪肝色、紫铜色、梨皮色、天青色、墨绿色等，并且有着很好的透气性。紫砂器表面带有含蓄的光泽，使用的时间越久，就越如同玉器，形成温润的表层，具有"可养性"。因此，紫砂制成的文具同著名的紫砂壶一样，为文人、雅士所钟爱。紫砂文具包括造型各异的注水类文具，还有笔架、笔筒、臂搁等。清代康熙、雍正时期著名的制陶大家陈致远最善于以紫砂制作各类文房用具，他所制瓜果式文具精巧、逼真，楚楚有致。如笋形紫砂水丞，形似一个横卧的竹笋，笋箨的细密筋脉、笋壳上虫咬的痕迹都被刻画得惟妙惟肖，无论色泽还是造型，都与真笋无异。

陶瓷文具上的装饰工艺有刻花、印花、贴花、陶塑、瓷雕等。

刻花

即用刀在胎上刻出较深的花纹，使花纹带有层次感，然后上釉，入窑烧制。这种装饰方法流行于宋代的北方瓷窑。

- 紫砂桃式砚滴（清）
Peach-shaped Inkstone Water Dropper from Yixing Kiln (Qing Dynasty, 1616-1911)

- 紫砂南瓜式水丞（清）
Pumpkin-shaped Water Container from Yixing Kiln (Qing Dynasty, 1616-1911)

as a real bamboo shoot both in color and shape.

Decorative craftsmanship on porcelain stationery includes engraving and printing flowers, appliqué, pottery arts, porcelain carving, and so on.

• 东汉永和紫砂朱笔洗
Purple Clay Red Brush Washer with the Feature of Yonghe Period in the Eastern Han Dynasty

• 紫砂红笔洗
Purple Clay Red Brush Washer

剔花

即用刀在胎上剔掉花纹以外的部分，使花纹凸起。这种装饰方法流行于宋代的北方瓷窑。

Engraving Flowers Design

It means engraving deep flower patterns on the body with a knife to feature the tiers of the patterns and then glaze it and fire it in a kiln. This kind of method was popular in the northern porcelain kilns in the Song Dynasty.

Picking Flowers

This means to picking out the parts outside the patterns to make them protruding. It was popular in the northern porcelain kilns in the Song Dynasty.

Scratching Flowers

This means scratching shallow and smooth flower patterns on the undried surface of the base with bamboo or wood stick and then glaze and fire it in a kiln. It was popular in the northern porcelain kilns in the Song Dynasty.

Appliqué

It is also known as "molded appliqué decoration", which was mostly used on green porcelain in the Sui Dynasty (581-618) and the Tang Dynasty. With mud as raw material, appliqué makes flower patterns by stamping and molding, then

划花

以竹签或木签在尚未干透的胎上划出浅浅的、线条流畅的花纹，然后上釉，入窑烧制。这种装饰方法流行于宋代的北方瓷窑。

贴花

亦称"模印贴花"，隋唐时期的青瓷器多施以此装饰方法。即以胎泥为原料，用模印或模塑的方法制成各种花纹，用泥浆贴在胎上，然后施釉并入窑烧制。

还有一种特殊的贴花——贴金，即将金箔剪成所需形状，粘贴在胎上入窑烧制后，在其上涂一层薄釉，再次入窑烧制。陶瓷贴金的方法，唐代已有之，盛行于宋代和明代，清代以后被用描金的方法取代。

描金

将金箔研磨成粉，用加以牛胶或白芨糊的红矾调匀金粉，描绘于瓷器的表面，再在700摄氏度至800摄氏度的温度下烧制，然后用玛瑙石磨之，即呈现出黄金的光泽。这种装饰方法流行于清代。

pastes the clay on the base, glazes and fires it.

Another appliqué decoration is pasting gold. It means cutting the gold foil into needed shapes, pasting it on the base, firing it, glazing a thin layer and then firing it in the kiln again. Pasting gold on porcelain was already seen in the Tang Dynasty and prevailed in the Song Dynasty and the Ming Dynasty. Since the Qing Dynasty, it was replaced by the method of gold-trace.

Gold-trace

Gold-trace means grinding gold foil into powder, adding red vitriol with gelatin or Hyacinth bletilla paste, mixing them and painting them on the surface of porcelain, firing the porcelain at a temperature of 700-800 degrees Celsius and then polishing it by the agate stone, which will make the gold shine. This decorative method was popular in the Qing Dynasty.

Porcelain Carving

As one of the porcelain decorative methods, it started during the Qin Dynasty (221 B.C.-206 B.C.) and the Han Dynasty, and flourished in the Ming Dynasty and the Qing Dynasty.

瓷雕

即陶瓷装饰的一种，始自秦汉，盛于明清。文房用具上的瓷雕一般分为浮雕和镂雕。陶瓷浮雕表现为采用堆、贴、刻的技法，使陶瓷表面产生凸起的纹样，分为高浮雕和浅浮雕，也有两者结合的方法。陶瓷镂雕亦称"镂空""透雕"。纹样穿透器壁的是全镂，只刻到器壁一半或浅层的为半镂，亦可两者结合。

Porcelain carving on study appliances can be divided into relief and engraved sculptures. Porcelain relief is to stack, paste and cut to make out protruding patterns on the surface of the porcelain. There are high relief and bas-relief or the combination of both methods. Porcelain engraving is also known as "hollow engraving" or "openwork". If patterns penetrate the wall of the ware, it is the whole engraving; if it is only carved into half of the wall or a shallow layer, it is the half engraving. The two methods can also be combined.

> 玉

中国人自古崇尚玉，"君子无故，玉不去身"。玉自然天成、含蓄而内敛、温润而坚韧的特性与中国人的品性和审美情趣一致。中国的玉文化与传统文化融合在一起，"君子比德于玉"，即儒家的玉德学说。因此在文房清供中，以玉制品最为丰富，几乎涵盖了各种文具。

汉代许慎的《说文解字》载："玉，石之美者兼五德者。"玉指的是有坚韧的质地、晶莹的色泽、艳丽的色彩、致密的纹理组织、悠扬致远的声音的美石。因此，广义概念的玉不限于硬玉和软玉这两类，还包括琥珀、水晶、松石、孔雀石、芙蓉石、珊瑚等，凡符合上述五德者，都在玉的范畴之内。

玉文具最早出现在殷商时期，河

> Jade

Chinese people have the tradition of respecting jade and there is a saying that " Gentlemen will always carry their jade with them despite special conditions"; Jade is naturally made, modest and reserved, tender and tenacious, which meets Chinese people's characteristics and aesthetic taste. Chinese jade culture and traditional culture are closely integrated. Confucian doctrine advocates the virtues of jade and has the saying "gentlemen are as virtuous as jade". So jade stationery and bibelot in ancient studies are the most abundant and cover almost all kinds of stationery.

In *Shuowen Jiezi* (*Explaining and Analyzing Characters* was an early 2nd century Chinese dictionary from the Han Dynasty) which was written by Xu Shen in the Han Dynasty (206 B.C.-220A.D.), it recorded " jade is the beauty in stones

南安阳殷墟出土过刻字用的雕刀，商代妇好墓出土过调制颜料的调色盘，俱以碧玉制成。早期的玉文房用具多为青玉、青白玉所制，后来陆续出现了白玉、黄玉、岫玉、翡翠、琥珀、玛瑙、水晶、松石等材质的玉器。

"玉不琢，不成器"，每件玉文房用具都经过了工匠的雕琢，才完美地呈现在人们面前。"切、

- 白玉桃蝠纹印盒（清）
White Jade Seal Box with Peach and Bat Patterns (Qing Dynasty, 1616-1911)

- 翡翠圆形镇纸（清）
Emerald Round Paperweight (Qing Dynasty, 1616-1911)

and has five virtues." Jade refers to fine stones which are tough in character, crystal and bright in color, dense in texture organization and melodious in sound. Therefore, the broad concept of jade is not limited to the two types of jadeite and nephrite, it also includes amber, crystal, turquoise, malachite, ross quartz, corals, etc. Stones with the above five virtues all belong to jade.

Jade stationery first appeared in the Shang Dynasty (1600 B.C.-1046 B.C.). The carving knife which was excavated in Anyang Yin Ruins and the paint palette from the tomb of Fuhao in the Shang Dynasty are all made of jasper (green jade). The early jade study appliances were mostly made of green and green white jade, and later there appeared other types made of white jade, topaz, serpentine, emerald, amber, agate, crystal, turquoise, etc.

There is a saying "Jade must be cut and chiseled to make it a useful vessel." So each study appliance in ancient studies should be chiseled by craftsmen to show its perfect form to people. "Cutting, grinding, carving and polishing" are feature processing steps of jade. Jade producing processes include: choosing and examining materials to make full use

- 青玉莲瓣纹笔洗（清）
Blue Jade Brush Washer with Pattern of Lotus Petals (Qing Dynasty, 1616-1911)

- 白玉荷莲笔洗（清）
Lotus shaped White Jade Brush Washer (Qing Dynasty, 1616-1911)

- 玛瑙八仙水丞（近代）
Agate Water Container with Patterns of Legendary Eight Immortals (Modern Times)

- 墨玉椭圆梅花笔洗（明）
Black Jade Oval Brush Washer with Plum Blossoms Patterns (Ming Dynasty, 1368-1644)

磋、琢、磨"是玉器加工的特色做法。制作玉器的工艺流程为：选料、审料，以达到石尽其美的目的。设计，根据玉料的质地、光泽、颜色、透明度等特点量料取材，因材施艺。然后就是"切、磋、琢、磨"，这是工匠按照设计

of stones. Designing, means working out the best way to use the jade according to its quality, luster, color, transparency and other characteristics of the jade. Then comes the process of "cutting, grinding, carving and polishing". In this process, craftsmen make the jade materials into ware according to the design. Cutting

将玉料加工成器的工序。"切"就是开料、切料，要用无齿的锯加解玉砂将玉料分开；"磋"就是用圆锯加砂浆修治；"琢"就是用钻等工具钻孔、雕琢花纹，玉雕分为圆雕、浮雕、薄浮雕和透雕；"磨"是对玉料进行打磨、抛光上亮。

is to separate and cut the materials with toothless saws and jade sand; Grinding is to clip it with a circular saw plus mortar; Carving is to drill with drills and carve patterns. Jade sculptures can be divided into circular engraving, high reliefs, thin high reliefs and hollow reliefs; Polishing is to make jade materials bright.

- 《天工开物》中的琢玉图　宋应星（明）
  Illustration of Jade Carving in *Exploitation of the Works of Nature* (an Encyclopedia of Technology with Illustrations) by Song Yingxing (Ming Dynasty, 1368-1644)

金镶玉

中国古代的手工艺，以镶玉和嵌金最为精细。金镶玉就是利用错金工艺在玉器上雕出细线纹饰，然后嵌金丝或银丝，再对玉器进行打磨。这其中又当属薄胎压丝嵌宝的工艺最为难得。运用这种工艺的玉器，胎壁要薄如纸张，厚度仅在3毫米左右。有的薄胎玉器甚至可以漂浮在水面，俗称"水上漂"。就是在这样薄的玉器壁上，不但要压上金丝，还要嵌上宝石，可见工艺多么精致，器物多么精美。

Jade Ware with Inlaid Gold

In the arts and crafts of ancient China, inlaid jade and gold are the most elaborate. Jade ware with inlaid gold is made by the inlaying gold technique. It is to carve thin-line patterns on jade ware, embed purl and grind the jade ware. It is also called "embedding gold". In the process, carving lines and inlaying purl on thin ware are the most difficult. Jade ware walls are as thin as a piece of paper with a thickness of only about 3mm. Some jade ware with thin walls can even float on the water, which is commonly known as "floating ware". How delicate the craftsmanship is to carve lines and inlay precious stones! How exquisite the ware is!

- 薄胎压金丝嵌宝石榴瓶（清）
Jade Pomegranate-shaped Bottle with Carved Gold Lines and Inlaid Precious Stones (Qing Dynasty, 1616-1911)

> 漆

漆器工艺是中国一门古老的手工技艺。以漆涂在表面的器具就是漆器。漆器不但色泽鲜亮，光彩夺目，而且防腐、耐酸碱。早在商周时期，漆器技艺就已经达到了相当高的水准，除了作为礼器，漆器还是生活的日用品。各个朝代都有相当精美的漆器生产。文具中的漆器也有很多，如砚屏、笔筒、印盒、墨床、笔匣、文具盒等，并且还被运用了很多装饰手段，如戗金、嵌螺钿、百宝嵌、雕漆等。

戗金

在罩漆完成的漆器表面，用针或细刀刻画出较纤细的纹样，然后在刻画出的花纹中上漆，再填以泥金或

> Lacquer

Lacquerware art is ancient Chinese craftsmanship. It is to paint on the surface of different ware with lacquer. Lacquerware is not only bright and dazzling in color, but also anti-corrosive and acid and alkali proof. As early as in the Shang Dynasty (1600 B.C.-1046 B.C.) and the Zhou Dynasty (1046 B.C.-256 B.C.), lacquerware craft reached a very high level. Besides the use as ritual ware, it was also used for daily necessities. There are exquisite lacquer productions in different dynasties. Much stationery is made of lacquer, such as inkstone screens, brush containers, seal boxes, ink rests, brush boxes, stationery boxes, etc. Also many decorative methods are used, such as incising and filling gold, inlaying mother-of-pearl, carving, and inlaying multi-treasure objects.

金箔，使花纹露出金色的阴文即为戗金。填银丝或银箔则为戗银。

嵌螺钿

这是将贝壳磨成薄片，按图案的花纹做成各种形体，嵌饰在漆器上的一种装饰方法。镶嵌的螺钿有薄厚之分，选用薄如蝉翼的螺片镶

Incising and Filling Gold

It means carving and drawing delicate patterns on the surface of painted lacquerware with a needle or a thin knife. Then painting on the patterns and filling gold or gold foil present show designs cut in intaglio. Sometimes silver thread or silver foil is also filled.

• 百宝嵌九老观画插屏（清）
Multi-treasure Inlaid Lacquer Table Screen with the Design of Nine Old Men (Qing Dynasty, 1616-1911)

嵌为"软螺钿",选用较厚的螺片镶嵌为"硬螺钿"。

百宝嵌

即把宝石、珍珠、珊瑚、翡翠、玛瑙、象牙、螺钿等一些珍贵材料雕成山水、人物、树木、楼台、花草等,混合镶嵌在漆器上,利用其不同的色泽达到五彩斑斓的艺术效果。

雕漆

这是在平面漆胎上剔刻花纹的一种漆器工艺技法。由于雕漆大多用朱红色的大漆,故名"剔

Inlaying Mother-of-pearl

It means grinding seashells into thin slices, making out various shapes according to the designed patterns and inlaying them into lacquerware. There is thin or soft and thick or hard mother-of-pearl. It can be as thin as a cicada's wings.

Multi-treasure Inlay

It means carving the valuable materials such as precious stones, pearls, coral, jade, agate, ivory, mother-of-pearl into designs of landscapes, human figures, trees, houses, flowers, etc., and inlaying them into the surface of lacquerware, which makes use of different luster to achieve colorful artistic effects.

• 雕漆墨床(清)
Carved Lacquer Ink Rest (Qing Dynasty, 1616-1911)

雕漆印泥盒
Lacquer Seal Box

红""雕红漆"。雕漆常以木、铜为胎，在上面堆少则八九十层、多则一两百层漆，待干后施以雕刻，花纹隐现，使器物显得精美而华丽、典雅而庄重。根据器物通体髹漆的颜色不同，还有"剔绿""剔黑"等表现形式。而用两三种色漆在漆胎上有规律地逐层堆积起来至相当的厚度后，再用刀剔刻花纹的技法，因与其他雕漆的效果不一样，从刀口的断面可以看到不同的色层，故这种雕漆技法被称为"剔犀"。

Carved Lacquerware

This is a technique to carve flower patterns on a flat lacquer base. Since carved lacquerware is mostly painted crimson, hence the name "red carved lacquerware". With the wood or copper base, carved lacquerware is often painted at least 80 or 90 to at most 100 to 200 layers; after the paint is dry, it will be carved and patterns will conceal gleamingly, which makes the ware beautifully ornate, elegant and dignified. According to the different colors of paints on ware, there is also green and black carved ware. Another "*Tixi*"(carving) technique is different from others. It is to paint two to three colors layer-to-layer to a certain thickness, then carve patterns with a knife. In this way, different colored layers can be seen from the cut of blade, which creates different effects from other carving techniques.

> 石

以石材作为文房用具是很常见的，尤其是印章，以及可以起到镇纸和笔架作用的陈设品山子。

印章最主要的用材就是石。由于要用刀来篆刻印章，印章的石材就要具备易刻的特性。而且，由于印章要被经常使用，石材还要具备不容易磨损的硬度。能够用于治印的石材很多，但古代最著名的印石要数寿山石、青田石和昌化石这"印石三宝"。

寿山石因产于福建福州的寿山乡而得名，是中国著名的印石之一。宋代时，寿山石便被大量开采，并用于雕刻。大的寿山石用于文房中的陈设，小的则为文人、雅士手中的把玩之物，精美者则被作为贡品进献朝廷。元代末期，寿山

> Stone

It is common for study appliances to be made of stone, especially for seals as well as rockworks (*Shanzi*) displayed on desks that functioned as paperweights or brush racks.

Seals are mostly made of stone. Since a seal is engraved by a graver, it requires the stone to be suitable for engraving. Moreover, since a seal is to be used frequently, the stone should be solid and not easily abraded. Many kinds of stone are fit materials for seals, among which three are especially famous in ancient China, namely *Shoushan* Stone, *Qingtian* Stone and *Changhua* Stone, collectively referred to as the Three Seal Stones.

Shoushan Stone, one of the most famous seal stones in China, is named after its producing place Shoushan Town in Fuzhou, Fujian Province. It was already massively exploited and

石多用于刻印。从那时起，收藏寿山石印材和寿山石印纽成为历代文人中的风气。寿山石中的田黄石，因石质具备细、洁、润、腻、温、凝这印石之"六德"，被称为"印石之冠"，自古就有"一两田黄一两金"的说法，是文人梦寐以求的至宝。除了作为印材，寿山石还被制成各类文房用品，如水丞、水注、笔洗、笔架、山子等。

used for engraving in the Song Dynasty (960-1279). Bigger ones were carved into bibelots in the study, smaller ones for the literati to play with their hands, and exquisite ones presented as gifts to the imperial court. In the late Yuan Dynasty, *Shoushan* Stone was mostly used for engraving seals. Since then, it became a vogue among the literati to collect *Shoushan* Stone as raw material for seals, and seals made of *Shoushan* Stone. *Tianhuang* Stone, among the many *Shoushan* Stones, is the King of Seal Stones, for it is endowed with the Six Virtues of seal stones, namely genuineness, firmness, smoothness, oiliness, coolness and translucency. From of old, this stone has been regarded as an equivalent to gold, and is a priceless treasure that men of letters pursue even in their dreams. Besides serving as a material for seals, *Shoushan* Stone is also made into many other study appliances, like water container, pouring pot, brush washer, brush container and rockwork.

- 寿山石兽纽"乐琴书寿永年"印章（清）
Beast-knob Seal Made of *Shoushan* Stone with Characters meaning "to Enjoy Music and Books to Gain Longevity" (Qing Dynasty, 1616-1911)

- 田黄三联印（清）
Three-part Seal Made of *Tianhuang* Stone (Qing Dynasty, 1616-1911)

青田石因产于浙江青田县而得名。青田石石色丰富，有着美妙的花纹，具有纯、净、正、鲜、透、灵六相。纯，指石质细腻而温润；净，指无杂质；正，指有典雅之感；鲜，指光泽鲜艳；透，指具有冰一般透明的感觉；灵，指有生动、灵异之感。六朝时就有了青田石雕，此后青田石多用于水丞、笔山、笔洗等文房用具。青田石的雕刻技艺有浅刻、浮雕、圆雕和镂雕。明代中叶，青田石印章逐渐流行起来。文人和雅士认为，青田石

Qingtian Stone is produced in Qingtian County, Zhejiang Province, hence its name. It has various colors with elegant patterns, and boasts the Six Traits, namely smoothness, genuineness, elegance, brilliance, translucency and vividness. Smoothness means that the stone feels smooth and cool; genuineness means that it has no foreign substances mixed in it; elegance means that it displays in a refined and graceful way; brilliance means that it shines in vibrant colors; translucency means that it is almost transparent like ice; and vividness means that it seems mysterious and full

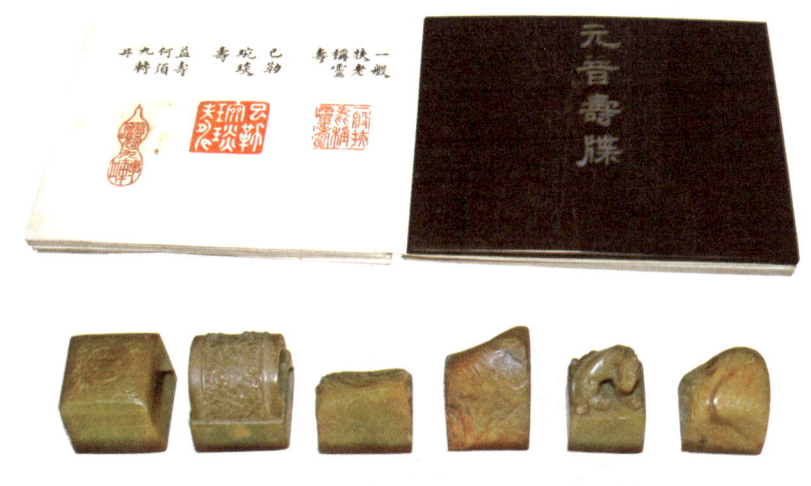

- 青田石"元音寿牒"组印（清）
  Qingtian Stone Seal Set with the Theme of "Honor Your Majesty's Longevity" (Qing Dynasty, 1616-1911)

• 鸡血石对章
Couple Seal Made of Bloodstone

以清新见长，象征隐逸、淡泊，故称其为"石中君子"。

昌化石产于浙江昌化，也称"昌化鸡血石"，因石材上分布有鲜艳的类似鸡血的红色斑块而得名。昌化石形成于1亿年前晚侏罗纪的流纹凝灰岩中，是朱砂在高岭石与迪开石之间不断渗染而成的。昌化石是中国"印石三宝"之一，是制作工艺品的上等材料。由于是一种罕见的珍奇之物，昌化石材的印石在清代极受皇家重视，如"乾隆之宝"御玺就是以昌化鸡血石制成的。

of life. Since the Six dynasties (the Wu of the Three Kingdoms, Eastern Jin, Song, Qi, Liang and Chen, 222-589), *Qingtian* Stone started to be used for carving, and later, it was mostly made into study appliances like water container, brush rack and brush washer. The techniques to engrave the stone include light engraving, relief, three-dimensional carving and piercing. In the middle of the Ming Dynasty, seals made of *Qingtian* Stone gradually gained popularity. The literati believed that *Qingtian* Stone stood out for its pureness which represented a sequestered life away from fame and wealth. Hence *Qingtian* Stone was titled the Noble Stone.

Changhua Stone is produced in Changhua, Zhejiang Province, and is also called *Changhua* Bloodstone, for it has red spots like chicken blood brightly scattered. The stone was formed in liparite through the flow of cinnabar between kaolinite and dickite in the Late Jurassic Period 100 million years ago. It is one of the Three Seal Stones in China and is first-tier material for other artifacts. Because of its rarity, *Changhua* Stone was already highly regarded by the imperial family in the Qing Dynasty (1616-1911). The seal of imperial seal

作为文房陈设品的石山子,多以自然形态的奇石,如灵璧石、英石、大理石、菊花石、孔雀石等制成。这些奇石自然崩落后,经过千百年的风化和流水的侵蚀,形成了千奇百怪的形状,其中玲珑而精巧者则被用于文房中书案上的陈设。

灵璧石是中国四大奇石之一,产于安徽灵璧,故名。灵璧石由大小均匀的微粒方解石组成,含有多种金属矿物质,叩之有声。灵璧石多为立体造型,有的肖形状景,有的气韵生动,是天然的艺术品。明代文震亨在《长物志》中写道:"石以灵璧为上……小者置几案间,色如漆声如玉者最佳。"清代乾隆皇帝誉之为"天下第一石"。

英石产于广东英德,与灵璧石同属沉积岩中的石灰岩。英石造型丰富,似峰峦起伏;多溶蚀特征,如洞穴幽深,表面则布满密而深的皱褶,有玲珑而精巧、奇雅而高绝的特点,在宋代就成为文房中案头上陈设的砚山。

菊花石形成于2.5亿至2.8亿年前,产于中国各地。菊花状图案不是由花的化石构成的,而是针状、柱状、纤维状的矿物呈放射状或束

Qianlong Zhi Bao (Qianlong's treasure), for example, was made of *Changhua* Bloodstone.

Stone rockworks, as furnishings in studies, are often made of peculiar stones in their natural forms, like *Lingbi* Stone, *Ying* Stone, *Dali* Stone, chrysanthemum stone and malachite. These unique stones, after parting from larger rocks and thousands of years of erosion by wind and water, are formed into all sorts of strange shapes. Among these, the most dainty and delicate ones serve as bibelots on desks in a study.

Lingbi Stone, one of the Four Peculiar Stones in China, is produced in Lingbi, Anhui Province, hence its name. It is constituted by granules of calcite with regular sizes, and contains many metal minerals and makes sounds upon knocking. Most *Lingbi* Stones are in a stereoscopic shape, some in a resemblance of certain objects or scenery, some graceful and vivid, making them born works of art. In his *Superfluous Things*, by Wen Zhenheng of the Ming Dynasty says, "*Lingbi* Stone rules among all stones… Small pieces are apt to be furnished on desks. Those that have colors like lacquer and sounds like jade are the best." Emperor Qianlong of the

• "春江水暖"灵璧石山子
Lingbi Stone Rockwork with the Theme of Water Warms in a Spring River

• "龙马拂波"英石山子
Ying Stone Rockwork with the Theme of Loong-horse Caroming Waves

状排列而形成的。这是在长期的地质变迁中，围岩中的碳酸钙成分围绕硅质燧石核而形成的立体放射状的结晶。最常见的菊花石表现为黑底白花的形式，花瓣为多层状，具

Qing Dynasty honored it as "the best stone in the world".

Ying Stone is produced in Yingde, Guangdong Province. As with *Lingbi* Stone, it is characterized as limestone, a kind of sedimentary rock. *Ying* Stone comes in plenty of shapes, just like layers of mountains. It is largely characterized by corrosion, which ends in seemingly deep holes. On the surface, there are many dense and deep drapes, cute, elegant, exotic and fantastic. It was ink rockworks on desks in a study in the Song Dynasty.

Chrysanthemum stone was formed 250-280 million years ago, and is found throughout China. The patterns of chrysanthemums are not made of fossils of chrysanthemums. Instead, they are needle-like, columnar or fiber-like minerals arranged in a radial or bunch-like way. They are formed in the long term of geological changes, when calcium carbonates in wall rocks crystallize in a radial pattern around siliceous paramoudras. The most commonly seen chrysanthemum stone features a black background with white flowers which have multilayer petals, forming a stereoscopic impression. The flowers vary in size and shape, yet all are

"前途无量" 菊花石山子
Chrysanthemum Stone Rockwork with the Theme of a Boundless Future

vivid and special.

Dali Stone is named after its producing place Dali, Yunnan Province. It is a kind of white limestone with black and brown patterns. The section plane of it is almost a Chinese wash painting. In ancient China, *Dali* Stones with set patterns were often selected to create decorative screens or to inlay into furniture. In addition, *Dali* Stone is a traditional material for artistic carvings of artifacts, study appliances, lamps, kitchen ware and other pragmatic objects as well as for architecture.

The name for malachite in Chinese is Peacock Stone literally, for it is similar in color with the green color of peacock

有立体感；花朵大小不一，花形各异，显得生动而奇特。

大理石因产于云南大理而得名。这是一种白色中带有黑色、褐色等花纹的石灰岩，从剖面看去，就像一幅水墨山水画。中国古代人常选取带有成形花纹的大理石来制作画屏或镶嵌在家具上。另外，大理石还是艺术雕刻的传统材料，

大理石挂屏
Hanging Screen Made of *Dali* Stone

可被雕刻成工艺品，以及文具、灯具、器皿等实用品，或被加工成建筑石材。

孔雀石颜色酷似孔雀羽毛上的绿色，故名。它产于铜的硫化物矿床氧化带，是原生含铜矿物氧化后形成的表生矿物，呈不透明的深绿色，有着色彩浓淡相间的条状花纹。在中国古代，孔雀石被称为"绿青""石绿"，除了可以做成各种装饰品和摆件，还是中国画颜料的原料。

leathers. It is found in the oxidation zone with cupreous sulfide deposits, and is a supergene mineral formed after the oxidation of primary cupreous mineral. It has an opaque deep green color with light or dark stripes. In ancient China, malachite was called "green-blue" or "stone-green", and was used for various decorations and furnishings as well as material for pigments of Chinese paintings.

• 孔雀石山水人物纹插屏
Malachite Table Screen Carved with Hills, Waters and Figures

> 竹

竹在中国古代文人的眼里有着正直、清逸的气节，宁折不弯，开怀而大度，是高风亮节的君子的象征。而以竹制作的笔筒和臂搁更是重要的文房用具，在文人、雅士之中广为流行，以彰显他们高洁、脱俗、文雅的情趣。

> Bamboo

For literati in ancient China, bamboos were noted for their integrity, unyieldingness and generosity, which were symbols of a noble man. Therefore, bamboo-made brush containers and armrests became important study appliances, and were popular among the literary circle to demonstrate their unsullied, refined and elegant taste.

Bamboo-made objects were found in as early as the Neolithic Age, and in the Jin Dynasty (265-420), bamboo brush containers came into being. The practice of carving on bamboo-made objects originated at a very early age, and was found throughout the

• 竹透雕荷叶纹笔筒（清）
Bamboo Brush Container with Openwork Carving of Lotus Leaves (Qing Dynasty, 1616-1911)

- 竹雕笔筒（清）
  Carved Bamboo Brush Container
  (Qing Dynasty, 1616-1911)

- 竹雕笔筒（清）
  Carved Bamboo Brush Container
  (Qing Dynasty, 1616-1911)

　　新石器时代就有了竹子制品，晋代时出现了竹制笔筒。在竹制的器物上进行雕刻起源颇早，历朝历代均有。而到了明代中叶之后，竹刻工艺更得到了很大的发展，特别是到了明代晚期，竹刻艺术形成了著名的金陵派和嘉定派。此时竹刻名家辈出，竹雕的笔筒和臂搁由仅为实用之物而向实用与欣赏兼备的类型转变，并逐渐成为文人、雅士的心爱之物。这些竹雕文房用具有的古朴、典雅，有的光素、大方，有的镂雕剔透，还有的色彩丰富，展现出不同的艺术效果。

　　在竹刻技艺上，除了有阴刻、

dynasties. After the middle of the Ming Dynasty, bamboo carving was rapidly developed, and particularly, two schools of bamboo carving, the Jinling School and the Jiading School, emerged in the late Ming Dynasty. At this moment, masters of bamboo carving appeared one after another, and bamboo-made brush containers and armrests were not only pragmatic, but also pragmatic and artistic at the same time. Thus, they were collected by the literati as beloved objects. Some of these carved bamboo appliances were archaic and graceful, some whitish and dignified, some delicately pierced and engraved, and some others vibrant and colorful, all

• 竹雕臂搁（近代）
Carved Bamboo Armrest (Modern Times)

• 竹雕臂搁（近代）
Carved Bamboo Armrest (Modern Times)

阳刻、透雕、圆雕、深浅浮雕、浮雕兼透雕等，还有留青、贴簧等工艺。这诸多工艺往往还同时被用在一件作品之上，手法甚为精妙；对于所雕刻的内容，凡山水、人物、

displaying different artistic effects.

Aside from intaglio and relief calligraphy cutting, openwork carving, three-dimensional carving, high and low relief, and relief with openwork carving, bamboo carving techniques also include skin carving and reed-pasting carving. One piece of work is often completed with more than one technique, and the skill is rather ingenious. The carved motifs cover landscapes, figures, flowers, grass and little animals, birds and beasts and stories, all of which are vivid and vigorous.

Skin carving is used when making armrests, paperweights, inkstone screens, brush containers and stationery cases. Skin carving is to carve the thin layer of the green bamboo skin into patterns, by removing the green skin that's not part of the pattern and exposing the inner part, hence the name skin carving, or green retaining carving. The green outer coating of the bamboo is as smooth as jade with light color, and turns light yellow with age. The inner part is fibrous and its color grows darker as time goes on and gradually turns dark red. Thus, with the differences in color and texture, distinctive layers are differentiated. Zhang Xihuang, a bamboo carving master in the late Ming Dynasty and

花卉、草虫、飞禽、走兽及故事题材，无不生动而有致。

留青竹刻制品有臂搁、镇纸、砚屏、笔筒、文具匣等。留青竹刻即在竹子表面的一层青皮（竹筠）上雕刻图纹，然后铲去图纹以外的青皮，露出下面的竹肌，故称"留青"，也叫"皮雕"。竹筠光润如玉，色浅，但年久便会变得微黄；竹肌有丝纹，年代越久，色越深，渐成红褐色。留青竹刻即利用这种色泽和质地的差异分出浓淡层次。明末清初的竹刻大家张希黄就是以留青技法独树一帜。他巧妙地利用被留青皮的竹子的薄厚变化，将图案的层次拉开，浮雕的层次达到

early Qing Dynasty, developed a style of his own with this skin carving technique. He skillfully made use of the variations in the thickness of what he removed from the bamboo to create different layers in the pattern. The relief might have five or six layers, with intaglio and relief elements, and abstract and concrete details all existing together harmoniously. The sunken and raised parts only subtly and precisely varied in thickness, making the whole image peaceful and profound, exhibiting marvelous carving skills.

Reed-pasting carving is also called reed-turning carving or *Wenzhu*. A moso bamboo is first cut into tubes whose knots and green skins are stripped away, leaving only a thin layer of bamboo reed.

• 留青竹刻笔筒（近代）
Green Retaining Bamboo Carving Brush Container (Modern Times)

• 竹雕《兰亭序》笔筒　王梅邻（清）
Bamboo Writing Brush Container Carved with the Inscription of *the Orchid Pavilion*, by Wang Meilin (Qing Dynasty, 1616-1911)

五六层，阴阳相配，虚实相生，凹凸变化精微，使器物有幽静、深远之感，显示出卓越的雕刻技巧。

贴簧竹刻也有"翻簧""文竹"等称法。具体做法是将毛竹锯成竹筒，去竹节和青皮，只留下一层很薄的竹簧（竹肌），经煮、晒、压平后，胶合或镶嵌在木胎、竹片上，然后磨光，再在上面雕刻纹样。因多在很薄的竹簧上施以雕刻，故以线刻或浅刻的阴刻为主。贴簧的制品色泽光润，类似象牙，以文具盒、笔筒为主，画面内容有山水、人物、花鸟、书法等。

After being boiled, dried and pressed flat, the bamboo reed is then pasted or inlaid onto a wooden blank or a bamboo chip. It is then polished and carved with patterns. Since the carving is conducted on rather thin bamboo reeds, the main techniques applied are line carving and shallow intaglio. Such artworks have a smooth and shiny surface like ivory, and are generally in the form of stationery receptacles and brush containers. Patterns carved include landscapes, figures, flowers and birds, and calligraphies.

嘉定派与金陵派

明代是竹雕工艺的成熟期，特别是明中叶之后，大部分竹刻高手都集中在江苏嘉定和金陵一带，并逐渐形成了以浮雕和圆雕著称的嘉定派和以浅刻见长的金陵派。

在嘉定派中，以创始人朱鹤为代表的祖孙三代最为著名。朱鹤，号松邻。因善书画，通古篆，所以在竹雕设计和制作中经常以笔法运用于刀法之中，创造出了竹雕的深刻法，即在竹上雕刻出五六层的镂空透雕。他制作的笔筒、香筒、臂搁、佛像等深受当时士人赞誉，人们往往不呼器名，而是直接以"朱松邻"称之。其子朱缨，即朱小松，为明代隆庆、万历时的竹刻名家，所刻的古仙、佛像为人称道。时人道："能世父业，深得巧思，务求精诣。"朱鹤之孙朱三松的竹刻技艺更臻绝妙，所刻笔筒及臂搁、小摆件名重一时。当时，嘉定派中有名的竹刻家达八七十人之多，对后世影响深远。

金陵派竹雕的创始人是濮澄，字仲谦，也是明代著名的竹刻家。与嘉定派竹刻"高、深、透"的风格不同，濮澄通常以浅刻技法来刻制竹笔筒、臂搁之类的文房器物。这种技法也被他用在木、牙、角等材料上。他尤其喜欢盘根错节的竹根，根据竹材的自然形状和特征施刻，在简洁的刀法的基础上略施雕凿，便自然成器。他用竹根雕出的器物曾妙绝一时，受到世人的喜爱。

Jiading School and Jinling School

The Ming Dynasty (1368-1644) is the maturation period for bamboo carving. In particular, in the latter half of the Ming Dynasty, the most proficient bamboo carving masters centered in the Jiading and Jinling areas of Jiangsu. Gradually, there emerged two schools, namely Jiading School, famous for its relief and three-dimensional carving, and Jinling School, famous for its light engraving.

In the Jiading School, the most famous masters are the three generations of the Zhu family, represented by its founding father Zhu He. Zhu He, also named Songlin, had a good knowledge of calligraphies, paintings and ancient seal script (a style of Chinese calligraphy). Therefore, in his bamboo carving designs and creations, he often applied writing techniques when carving with a graver, thus inventing the deep carving technique, i.e., carving out five or six layers of hollowed-out openwork carving. The brush containers, incense containers, armrests and Buddha figures that he made were highly regarded by contemporary literary people. The objects were addressed often not with their names, but directly as Zhu Songlin. His son Zhu Ying, also named Zhu Xiaosong, was a bamboo carving master in the Longqing Period (1567-1572) and Wanli Period (1573-1620) in the Ming Dynasty. He was praised for carving mythological immortals and Buddha figures. Contemporary comment goes like this: "He's able to inherit his father's cause, understanding the exquisite philosophy and pursuing the utmost accuracy." Zhu He's grandson Zhu Sansong was even more exceptionally skilled at bamboo carving. His brush containers, armrests and bibelots were highly renowned for a time. In the Jiading School, there were as many as sixty or seventy famous bamboo carving masters at that time, who profoundly influenced later times.

The founder of the Jinling School Pu Cheng, whose style name is Zhongqian, was another bamboo carving master in the Ming Dynasty. Different from the "high, deep and hollow" style of Jiading School, Pu Cheng often adopted a relief technique that was carved in a very light way to decorate brush containers, armrests and other appliances. This technique was also applied when dealing with materials like wood, ivory and horn. He liked twisted and coiled bamboo roots in particular, and carved in accordance with the natural shape and traits of the bamboo. With simple and light carvings, the bamboo became a work of art at ease. The objects that he carved out of bamboo roots were superb for some time and gained popularity.

> 木

中国古人一向追求"和谐"，强调"天人合一"。儒家和道家认为，"天"为大，是自然之本，而人要取法于自然、融合于自然，与自然和谐。木生长于自然，源于"盛木为怀"的理念，古代文人因而对木制的文房用具情有独钟。木制的文房用具，如笔筒、臂搁、笔架、墨床、文具盒等，均以佳木为材，如黄花梨木、紫檀木、黄杨木、沉香木、红木等，并采用了雕刻、镶嵌、拼制等装饰技法，不仅制作工艺精湛，而且很好地展现了木材独特的美感。

黄花梨木质地细腻，为黄褐色，纹理若隐若现，结疤之处有铜钱大小的圆晕形花纹。由于其木质自然而美观、温润而光滑、坚固而

> Wood

Ancient Chinese people always sought the state of harmony, emphasizing the organic integration of man and nature. It was believed by Confucianism and Taoism that *Tian* was a larger being than man and was the foundation of nature; whereas man should seek law and philosophy from nature, integrate with nature and live in harmony with nature. Trees grew in nature, so the ancient literati, who embraced the idea of "luxuriant trees are a symbol of man's broad mind", had a special preference for wood study appliances. Brush containers, armrests, writing brush racks, ink rests, stationery receptacles and other wood appliances are made with first-rate woods like scented rosewood, padauk, boxwood, eaglewood, mahogany, etc., using such techniques as carving, inlaying, and joining. They are created with exquisite

耐腐，且香气持久，成为制作贵重家具和实施雕刻工艺的上等木材。明清时期，有着含蓄、内敛的君子风范的黄花梨木笔筒最负盛名。

紫檀木呈紫黑色，紫色在中国古代有祥瑞之寓意。紫檀木木形优良，但由于生长缓慢，数量非常稀少，民间有"百年寸檀"之说。紫檀木木质坚硬而厚重，纹理细腻，耐腐、耐久；紫色的纹理中夹杂着黑色的线条，色彩美观而庄重。以紫檀木制作的笔筒、臂搁等文房用具，在明、清两代成为宫廷中的收藏珍品。

craftsmanship, and moreover, represent the unique beauty that wood alone expresses.

Scented rosewood is yellowish-brown, dense in texture, and the grains are partly hidden and partly visible. Around the knots, there are circular patterns about the size of a copper coin. It features an unaffected and pleasing appearance, mild, gentle and smooth feel, firm wood that resists corrosion, and lasting fragrance. All of these make the scented rosewood a superior material for furniture and carving. In the Ming Dynasty (1368-1644) and the Qing Dynasty (1616-1911), brush containers

- 紫檀木笔筒（清）
Padauk Brush Container (Qing Dynasty, 1616-1911)

- 紫檀雕花卉笔筒（清）
Padauk Brush Container Carved with Flowers (Qing Dynasty, 1616-1911)

红木木质坚硬，耐用，呈深红色或黑红色，纹理光滑而细密。清代时，红木除了被用作制作家具，还多被制成文具箱、书匣、砚屏、文具架等文房用具。

沉香又称"奇楠香"，心材为著名熏香原料，产于印度、泰国、越南等地。据称，它分泌的脂膏凝结为块，入水能沉，故名"沉香"。沉香在中国历来是较为珍贵的木材之一，除用作香料，也用来

made of this wood, an emblem of a reserved and self-restrained noble man, enjoyed the highest reputation.

Padauk is purplish black, and purple signifies luck and auspice in ancient China. It is of high quality, yet grows rather slowly, which is exemplified in the folk saying "a hundred years an inch," indicating the rarity of padauk. The wood is solid, thick and dense, and free from corrosion even in a long time. Its purple patterns are mixed with black lines, making it charming and solemn. In the Ming Dynasty and the Qing Dynasty, study appliances made of padauk, such as brush containers and armrests, were treasures collected in the imperial palace.

Mahogany is of hard wood and stands wear and tear. It may be russetish or black red, and its texture is smooth and close. In the Qing Dynasty, mahogany is not only used for making furniture, but also for study appliances like stationery boxes, book cases, inkstone screens and stationery racks.

Eaglewood, also called sinking wood in Chinese, grows mainly in India, Thailand and Vietnam. The middle part of the wood is a famous material for spice. It is recorded that its grease, when congealed, may sink down into water,

- 沉香木笔筒（明）
Eaglewood Brush Container (Ming Dynasty, 1368-1644)

制作文房器具、家具饰件、小型工艺品等。

黄杨木呈红褐色，质地坚密，肌理细腻而柔润。人们取其天然的优美形态，以起伏、盘曲形成的凹陷处作搁笔之用，不加任何雕饰，古朴、自然、浑然天成。

hence the name sinking wood. Eaglewood has long been a precious kind of wood in China, and is used for, besides spices, study appliances, decorative objects on furniture and other little works of art.

Boxwood is dark red. It has a firm and thick texture and the grains feel smooth and gentle. It is unpretentiously elegant, and the hollow parts formed by the rise and fall of its waving grains happen to be appropriate for resting brushes. Such racks are unaffected, archaic and natural as an integral whole.

- 黄杨木雕雀梅笔筒（现代）
Boxwood Brush Container Carved with Sparrows and Plum Blossoms (Modern Times)

- 黄杨木随形笔架（清）
Natural Boxwood Brush Rack (Qing Dynasty, 1616-1911)

> 象牙

象牙色白，细润而光滑，有着天然的纹理，质地坚硬而富有韧性，适于雕刻成精美的饰物和器物。不仅在中国，世界上文明发展较早的人类社会都有制作象牙雕刻品的历史。在中国，早在距今7000年至距今4000年的新石器时代，就出现了象牙制品。在周代，象牙与珠、玉、石、木、金、皮革、羽毛一起被列为制作王室礼器、珍玩的"八材"之一。在秦代，象牙制品与昆山之玉、明月之珠、夜光之璧相提并论，成为王公贵族、文人、雅士地位和财富的象征。在唐代的文房用具中，出现了十分精美的拨镂象牙尺。当时的象牙雕刻盛行以线刻作为装饰，时称"拨镂"，就是用刻刀在染了色的象牙上进行浅

> Ivory

Ivories are charmingly white, feel slick and glossy, and have natural grains. They are solid with tenacity, and are apt to be carved into fancy jewlry and other objects. Not only in China, but many other peoples that have a long civilization have a history of making ivory carvings. Ivory-made objects in China can be traced back to as far as 7,000 to 4,000 years from today in the Neolithic Age. In the Zhou Dynasty (1046 B.C.-256 B.C.), ivories, as with pearls, jades, stones, woods, gold, leathers and feathers, were regarded as one of the Eight Materials for imperial rite instruments and rare curios. In the Qin Dynasty (221 B.C.-206 B.C.), ivory objects enjoyed the same status as jades from Kunlun Mountains, bright-moon pearls and round jades shining at night, symbolizing the status and wealth of the royal family and the

• 象牙臂搁（近代）
Ivory Armrests (Modern Times)

• 象牙笔筒（清）
Ivory Brush Container (Qing Dynasty, 1616-1911)

literati. Exquisitely-made ivory rulers that were dyed and carved were found in study appliances in the Tang Dynasty (618-907). The technique applied to carve ivories at that time is called *Bo Lou*, which means dyeing the ivories first and then carve them in a light way with a graver. The prevailing method in carving ivories is line carving. In the Song Dynasty (960-1279), the making of study appliances reached a peak. Ivory-made brush containers, brush racks, brush cases and table screens were indispensable articles in a study. In the Ming Dynasty (1368-1644) and the Qing Dynasty (1616-1911), ivory appliances were more delicately made, including brush dipping, brush container, brush rack, ink rest, armrest, paperweight, paper knife, album cover, seal, table screen and stationery receptacle. Besides line carving, many other techniques like relief, three-dimensional carving and piercing were adopted. In addition, special techniques like color smoking were applied, making the ivories even more exquisite beyond compare. They became more than practical, but were also of high artistic and appreciative values.

Many methods are used when

刻。宋代时，文房清供的发展达到鼎盛时期，象牙制的笔筒、笔架、笔匣、插屏等成为文房中不可或缺的用具。明、清两代，象牙笔舔、笔筒、笔架、墨床、臂搁、镇纸、纸刀、册页、印章、插屏、文具盒等文房用具被制作得更为精细，除了线刻，还采用了浮雕、圆雕、镂雕等多种技法，再加上彩熏等特殊工艺，这些象牙制品精美绝伦，除了具有实用性，还具有极高的艺术价值和欣赏价值。

象牙有多种装饰方法，如雕刻工艺、彩熏工艺、镶嵌工艺等，这些技法重工艺、重选料、重意境，集中体现了中国古代象牙雕刻的最高水平。

象牙雕刻工艺

此工艺又分线刻、圆雕、浮雕、镂空雕等。根据器物或题材的不同，这些雕刻技艺或浑厚、简练，或繁复、富丽，或灵动、飘逸，艺术水平至臻至善，巧夺天工。

象牙彩熏工艺

此工艺即给象牙上色，分熏黄和上彩两种。熏黄是根据时间的长

decorating ivories, like carving techniques, color-smoking techniques and inlaying techniques. These methods emphasize skills, materials and effects, representing the highest level of ivory carving in ancient China.

Ivory Carving Techniques

These techniques include line carving, three-dimensional carving, relief and

- 象牙屏风（清）
Ivory Screen (Qing Dynasty, 1616-1911)

piercing. Different techniques are applied when carving ivories of different styles and themes for different purposes. Some are vigorous and simple, some complex and gorgeous, some vivid and graceful. The artistic standards, marvelous and wonderful to excel nature, are at the peak of perfection.

• 象牙屏风（清）
Ivory Screen (Qing Dynasty, 1616-1911)

短故意将象牙制品做旧，可使象牙具有不同的古旧之颜色。上彩是用颜料对象牙制品的表面进行覆盖和涂染。上彩分半彩和整彩两类。半彩是仅对局部施彩，其余大部分为象牙本色；整彩是对象牙制品的所有部分都施彩绘。

象牙镶嵌工艺

就是用象牙料做成局部的装饰

• 象牙臂搁（近代）
Ivory Armrest (Modern Times)

部件，再以拼贴的方式将之镶嵌在器物上，也可以与玉、木材、金、银等材料一起镶嵌。还有一种包镶工艺，就是以木为胎，将象牙薄片包镶在木胎上。

Ivory Color-smoking Techniques

This is to change the original color of the ivories, and two techniques are used, namely yellow-smoking and painting. Yellow-smoking is to intentionally make ivories archaic. With different durations of the smoking process, the ivories will put on colors that may appear to be from ancient times. Painting is to cover or dye the ivory surface with pigments. It is divided into two types, partial painting and entire painting. The former is to paint only some parts of the ivory, leaving the rest with the original color; and the latter is to paint the ivory object from top to toe.

Ivory Inlaying Techniques

This is to make ivories into little decorative components and inlay them onto other devices with the joining method. Sometimes they are inlayed together with jade, wood, gold and silver. There is also a special technique called rim inlaying, which is to bind a thin piece of ivory around a wood blank.

- 象牙笔筒（近代）
  Ivory Brush Container (Modern Times)

- 象牙刻李白诗笔筒（清）
  Ivory Brush Container Carved with Li Bai's Poem (Qing Dynasty, 1616-1911)

> 匏

古人称葫芦为"匏",匏器则是以范制葫芦之法制成的。趁葫芦幼小,将之纳入以木或陶制的带有阴纹的模范中,待之长成后,经修整、漆里、加象牙等口边,即得各式有阳文花纹的器皿。此工艺颇为复杂,甚至有"百不得一"的说法,即在一百个用范制成的葫芦中,有一个成功就很难得了。

> Gourd

Gourds were called *Pao* by ancient Chinese people. With the method of gourd molding, they can be molded into various shapes. When a gourd is immature, a wood or pottery mold with intaglio patterns is covered outside of it. When it matures, the mold is removed, and after polishing, inner-painting, and ivory rim inlaying, a gourd device with various relief patterns comes into being. This technique is quite complex, which is supported by the saying "less than one out of a hundred", meaning that it is worth celebrating even to make one molded gourd useful out of a hundred.

- 匏制笔筒(清)
Gourd Brush Container (Qing Dynasty, 1616-1911)

● 传统文房书桌摆设 (图片提供：全景正片)
Traditional Stationery on Study Desk

附录：书房陈设品
Appendix: Antiques in Studies

　　古代文人的书房中除了文房用具，还陈设有许多古器。这些古玩包括书法、名画、碑帖、古铜器、古玉、古琴、明器、古瓷器等。文人们把在书房内鉴赏文玩看成是修身养性的典雅情趣，是最高的艺术享受。

Besides the study appliances, there are many antiques, and ancient craftworks displayed in the studies of literati, including works of calligraphy, famous paintings, inscription copybooks, ancient bronze wares, ancient jade, ancient seven-stringed zither (*Guqin*), funerary wares, ancient porcelains, etc. They consider appreciating antiques in studies as an elegant interest for self-cultivation, as well as the highest artistic feast.

古铜器

　　古铜器也称"钟鼎彝器""吉金"。古代的达官贵人、文人、雅士对古铜器的收藏可谓成癖，时时把玩、鉴赏，无不以文房内陈设有古铜器为荣耀。中国历代都出现过卓

- 葵式抚琴引凤铜镜（唐）
Petal-shaped Copper Mirror with the Theme of Playing Zither to Attract the Phoenix (Tang Dynasty, 618-907)

Ancient Bronze Ware

The ancient bronze ware is also called *Zhongding Yiqi* or *Jijin* in ancient China. The ancient nobles, literati were addicted to the collection of the ancient bronze ware. They would take them out to appreciate from time to time and were proud of their display of ancient bronze wares. So there appeared many distinguished collectors and masters in the study of inscriptions. They wrote books and set up a theory in the prevalence of textual research, like the *Note of Ancient Wares of the Pre-Qin Dynasty*, *Antique Collection of Xuanhe Period*, in the Song Dynasty (960-1279); the *Appreciation of Ancient Wares of the Western Qing, Fuzhai Jijin Lu*, in the Qing Dynasty (1616-1911), etc.

　　The ancient bronze ware includes the sacrificial vessels used in ritual ceremonies, like the cooking utensils,

• 铜制朝冠耳三足炉（清）
Three-legged Copper Stove with Official Hat's Ears (Qing Dynasty, 1616-1911)

such as the tripod, *Li* (an ancient cooking vessel with hollow legs), *Gui* (an ancient two-eared cooking vessel used for storing rice), *Fu* (caldron), etc.; and the drinking vessel, such as *Jue*, *You*, *Gu*, Gong (an ancient wine vessel made of horn), *Fang Yi*, *Zun*, etc.; and the musical instruments, such as bell, bronze drum, and little bell, etc. Additionally, there are bronze weapons including knife, sword, battle-axe (*Yue*), halberd, etc. Especially the copper mirror and stove were collected by literati in a large scale and became an inevitable display in the study.

Ancient Jades

Since ancient times, the Chinese have had the tradition of collecting jade articles. The ancients believed that the jade is the spirit of the heaven and the earth, as well as the essence of the sun and the moon. They also believed that it can not only be used to bless with safeness, but also be a symbol of good fortune. Several jade articles were unearthed from the Red Mountain Cultural Relics (five or six thousand years ago). Each historical stage has some remains of ancient jade ware which has the characteristics of the times. Many of the emperors in China were

有成就的大收藏家和金石学家，他们纷纷著书立说，考据之风大盛，如宋代的《先秦古器记》《宣和博古图》，清代的《西清古鉴》《簠斋吉金录》等。

古铜器包括商周时期举行祭祀活动的礼器。包括饪食器，如鼎、鬲、簠、釜等；酒水器，如爵、卣、觚、觥、方彝、尊等；乐器，如钟、铜鼓、铃等。除此之外，还有青铜制作的兵器，如刀、剑、钺、戟等。特别是铜镜和铜炉，更为历代文人所珍藏，成为文房中不可或缺的陈设。

古玉

中国人自古以来就有收藏玉器的风尚。古人认为，玉为天地之灵、日月之精，有保平安的作用，是祥瑞的象征。距今五六千年的红山文化遗址就有玉器出土，每个历史时期都有一些富有时代文化特征

- 白玉墨床（清）
  White Jade Ink Rest (Qing Dynasty, 1616-1911)

- 白玉墨床（清）
  White Jade Ink Rest (Qing Dynasty, 1616-1911)

interested in collecting ancient jade, thus the jade became the important symbol of feudalist etiquette, the authority, the social status and wealth. Also, there are many books about the collection and the research of the ancient jade.

The favorite ancient jade ware of the ancient literati includes jade *Bi* (referring to a flat and round-shaped jade that has a tiny hole in it), jade *Cong* (referring to a tube shaped jade that is squared outside and round inside), jade *Gui* (referring to a rectangular jade), jade *Hu* (referring to a jade ware which is tiger-shaped), jade *Zhang* (referring to a flat, rectangular jade), jade *Huang* (referring to a curved shaped jade) and other ritual objects; and jade belt, jade pendant and other decorated jade ware; jade *Wo* (referring to the jade which was gripped by a dead people in the hands), jade *Sai* (referring to the jade which was used to be filled in the eyes, nostrils, ears, mouth, genitals and anus), jade *Hanchan* (referring to the jade was produced into the shape of a cicada) and other funeral objects, as well as jade figure, jade sword ornaments, jade animal, jade vessels and other jade displays. Some of them can not only be used for decoration, but also can be used as study appliances like ink rests and penholders.

的古玉遗存。中国历代的君王中有很多喜好收藏古玉，古玉成为封建礼制、权力、地位和财富的重要标志。古代关于古玉收藏和研究的论著更是比比皆是。

古人喜爱的古玉主要包括玉璧、玉琮、玉圭、玉琥、玉璋、玉璜等礼器，玉带、玉佩等佩玉，玉握、玉塞、玉含蝉等葬玉，玉人，玉剑饰、玉兽、玉器皿，以及各种玉摆件。其中有些古玉制品除了用于陈设，还可以被当作文房用具使用，如作为墨床、笔架等。

"古泉"

人们称中国古代的钱币为"古泉"。古钱币承载了大量的文化信息，是中国历史文化的重要遗存，有着极高的文化价值和艺术价值。因此，古代的文人、雅士对古钱币的收藏、把玩和鉴赏十分热衷。中国是世界上最早使用铸币的国家，古钱币历史久远。从原始社会的贝币，到殷商晚期以青铜仿贝壳形态的"无文铜贝"，及至春秋战国时期已确立的布币、刀币、蚁鼻钱和

Ancient Coin

The ancient Chinese coin was called ancient *Quan*. It carries vast cultural information and is an important relic of Chinese history and culture, possessing a high cultural value and aesthetical value.

- 方孔圆钱 "开元通宝"（唐）
Circular Coin with a Square Hole: Kaiyuan Tongbao (Tang Dynasty, 618-907)

- 元宝形银锭（清）
Shoe-shaped Silver Ingot (Qing Dynasty, 1616-1911)

圜钱四大货币体系，再到秦始皇统一六国后改铸的圆形方孔钱，历朝、历代都铸有自己的钱币。

　　古钱币的种类非常丰富，形制多样，制作材料繁多。按照材质，主要分为贝币、金属币和纸币。金属币又分为金银钱、铜钱、铁钱、铅钱等。

　　按照形制的不同，古钱币可以分为贝币、布币、刀币、蚁鼻钱、圜钱、方孔圆钱等。

　　按照命名方式的不同，古钱币还可以分为铸有重量的记重钱、铸有价值或对银比价的记值钱、铸有皇帝年号的年号钱、铸有铸造年份的记年钱、铸有铸钱局或铸钱地点的记地钱等。

古印

　　印章在中国已有两三千年的历史，古代文人热衷于印玺的收藏、鉴别和研究。古代印玺大多为玉、金、银、铜所制，包括了鸟篆、大篆、小篆等各种字体。古印上的印文和印纽显示了精湛的雕刻技法。很多古印被收录成图谱，成为金石学

So the ancient literati were addicted to the collection and appreciation of ancient coins. The development of ancient coins has a long history. And China is the first country in the world to use the foundry coin. From the earliest shell coin in the primitive society, the character-less bronze shell coin in the late Shang Dynasty, the Four-coin System established in the Eastern Zhou Dynasty (770 B.C.-256 B.C.) namely the spade-shaped coin, knife-shaped coin, *Yibi* coin and round coin, to the unified circular coin with a square hole cast in the Qin Dynasty (221 B.C.-206 B.C.) after the unification of the whole country, each dynasty had its own coin.

　　The ancient coin is varied in kind, type and material. According to its material, it can be categorized into shell coins, metal coins and paper notes. And the metal coin can be further sorted into gold and silver coin, copper coin, iron coin and lead coin.

　　According to the differences of the type, the ancient coin can be classified as a shell-shaped coin, spade-shaped coin, knife-shaped coin, *Yibi* coin, round coin, circular coin with a square hole, etc.

　　According to the naming pattern, the ancient coins can be categorized into the

• 牙雕"马上封侯"纽印章（清）
Ivory Carving Seal with the Theme of Granted on the Horse Back (Qing Dynasty, 1616-1911)

• 牙雕八宝纽印章（清）
Ivory Carving Seal with the Theme of Eight Treasures (Qing Dynasty, 1616-1911)

的重要方面。商代的青铜古玺奇异多姿，有巨玺和多形玺，为后来的印章款式提供了多元化的范式；字体或夸张变形，或细致而严密。秦代时，肖形印别具神采，字体以小篆为正统，形成了质朴而雄健的风格。以汉

weight-marked coin, rate-marked coin (marked with exchange rate with silver), period-marked coin (marked with the cast period), year-marked coin (marked with the production year) and the bureau-marked coin (marked with its cast bureau), etc.

Ancient Seal

The Chinese seal already has a history of two or three thousand years. The ancient literati were addicted to the collection, identification and research of ancient seals. The ancient seal is mainly made of jade, gold, silver and copper, with the inscription of various styles like the bird seal script, large seal script, small seal script, etc. The inscriptions and seal knot indicate the distinguished carving techniques. Many ancient seals are collected in illustrated catalogues which are an important part of the study of inscriptions. The bronze seal of the Shang Dynasty (1600 B.C. 1046 B.C.) is varied in style, including the giant seal and multi-form seal, which provide a diversified normal form for the successive seal. The style of the character is either exaggerated and deformed or delicate and regular. In the Qin Dynasty, the picture seal stood out. The character

代为代表，包括三国、两晋、南北朝的"汉印"，集前人之大成，印章品类之多、创作之美，成为治印史上的一个高峰。唐宋时期开创了斋馆印的先河。元代，画家王冕首以花乳石刻印，结束了以往借鉴硬材质，文人难以自制印章的历史。明、清两代，治印名家辈出，在借鉴秦汉印精华的基础上，还吸取了金石类文字的营养，打造出了印章的辉煌时期。

瓦当

瓦当是中国古代建筑的重要构件，是铺设在屋檐最前端的一片瓦。其样式主要有圆形和半圆形两种，主要功能是防水、排水、保护

- 半圆形饕餮纹瓦当（战国）
  Semicircular Ancient Eaves Tile with *Taotie* (A Mythical Ferocious Animal) Motif (Warring States Period, 475 B.C.-221 B.C.)

style was restricted to the small seal script and formed a plain and powerful feature. The Han's seal represented by the seals in the Han Dynasty (206 B.C.-220 A.D.), the Three Kingdoms Period (220-280), the Jin Dynasty (265-420), as well as the Southern and Northern dynasties (420-589), inherited the advantages of the former styles. The diversification and beauty of the seal became a peak in the seal production in China. In the Tang Dynasty (618-907) and the Song Dynasty, the study seal started to prevail. By the Yuan Dynasty (1206-1368), the famous painter Wang Mian had been the first man to carve seal out of a dolomite, which ended the history when the literati could not make seals by themselves due to the hardness of the raw material. In the Ming Dynasty (1368-1644) and the Qing Dynasty, masters of seal production came forth in large numbers. On the basis of absorbing the essence of the seal in the Qin Dynasty and the Han Dynasty, they also referred to the study of inscriptions and created a glorious time of seal production.

Ancient Eaves Tile

The ancient eaves tile is an important part

• 圆形云纹瓦当（汉）
Round Ancient Eaves Tile with Cloud Motif (Han Dynasty, 206 B.C.-220 A.D.)

木制飞檐和美化屋面轮廓。古代文人喜欢收藏秦代和汉代的瓦当，将之作为文房内的玩赏之物。秦代的瓦当以纹饰居多，有动物纹、几何纹、植物纹、云气纹等，动物纹有"四灵"（青龙、白虎、朱雀、玄武）、鹿、鸿雁、鱼等。汉代的瓦当基本以灰陶为主，多为装饰有篆体文字的瓦当。文字瓦当分为标名类和吉祥语类。标名类表现为在瓦当上写明建筑物的名称，即宫殿、官署、陵园之名。吉祥语类瓦当上有"延年益寿""长生无极""千秋万岁""永寿无疆"等表达人们

for traditional Chinese architectures. It indicates the tiles paved on the front end of eaves, with two main types of round and semicircle. It is primarily used for waterproof function, drainage, protection for the wooden overhanging eaves and decoration of roofing contour. In the past, literati were fond of collecting the ancient eaves tiles of the Qin Dynasty and the Han Dynasty as antiques which could be displayed in their studies. Eaves tiles of the Qin Dynasty are mainly decorated with various motifs involving the themes of animals, geometric patterns, plants, cloud and air patterns, etc., among which the animal motifs include the Four Auspicious Animals (referring to Blue Loong, White Tiger, Red Phoenix, Black Tortoise), deer, swan goose and fish, etc. However, eaves tiles of the Han Dynasty are mainly made of grey pottery and decorated with the inscriptions of seal characters. The inscription tile has two kinds, designation and auspicious greeting. The former one has the architecture's name engraved on it, which is the name of the palace, government office and cemetery. The latter one is carved with auspicious greetings like longevity, limitlessness, everlasting kingship, eternity and boundlessness.

附录：书房陈设品 Appendix: Antiques in Studies

祈求吉祥的文字。瓦当上的字体用笔抑扬顿挫，为历代书法家和篆刻家所珍重，他们常模拟瓦当风格入书、入印。

古瓷器

不限于文房诸具，书房内往往还陈设有历朝、历代的古瓷器，这在很大程度上反映了书房主人的审美情趣和品位。古瓷器至今仍是文人们首选的书房收藏品，蕴藏着深厚的文化底蕴和人文内涵。

- 景德镇窑绿地金彩云龙纹瓶（清）
Gold-traced Green Glazed Vase with Cloud and Loong Pattern, from Jingdezhen Kiln (Qing Dynasty, 1616-1911)

- 天蓝釉瓜棱双耳蒜头瓶（清）
Azure Glazed Two-eared Garlic Vase with Melon Ridges (Qing Dynasty, 1616-1911)

The Chinese characters on eaves tiles are written in a cadenced and unstrained way, so they were deeply cherished by generations of calligraphers and engravers who often imitated the character styles of the inscription tiles while compiling copybooks or engraving seals.

Ancient Porcelain

Aside from the stationery, there are also displays of the ancient porcelain ware in the study, which reflects the aesthetic taste of the owner to a great extent. The ancient porcelain ware has always been the top choice of the study collection, from which we can see the profound cultural deposits and human connotation.

• 碑帖
Inscription Copybook

碑帖

　　碑帖是碑版和法帖的简称，为石刻、木刻文字的拓本或印本，供临摹使用。"碑"指古代被刻凿在摩崖、碑、碣、墓和造像石上的石刻文字，多为书法名家或高手所书。用纸和墨将碑石上的字捶拓下

Inscription Copybook

The inscription copybook (*Beitie*, is the abbreviation of *Beiban* and *Fatie*, respectively indicating the rubbings of tablets and scripts of calligraphers), refers to the rubbing or the printed copy of inscriptions on stone or wood boards, which is used for imitating and studying of calligraphy. Tablets (*Bei*), are ancient stone inscriptions engraved on cliffs, steles, stone tablets, gravestones and statues, most of which were written by calligrapher masters. People make rubbings from inscriptions on stone tablets with paper and ink, and then compile them together into a book of rubbings. Copybooks (*Tie*), are books of rubbings compiled by the rubbings from inscriptions carved based on the scripts of famous calligraphers on stone or wooden boards. The inscription copybook is published for later generations to study. It was a major cultural transmission method at the early stage of the development of printing. Especially in the Qing Dynasty, the epigraphy thrived. Not only was the study of tablet rubbings highly valued, the researches of the inscriptions on bronze vessels of the Xia Dynasty (approx. 2070 B.C.-1600 B.C.), the Shang Dynasty and

来，再经装裱就成为拓本。"帖"指在石上或枣木板上将著名书法家的真笔墨迹镌刻、捶拓，汇集成的拓本。碑帖拓本是专供后人取法的，这在印刷术发展的前期是传播文化的重要手段。尤其在清代，金石学兴盛，不但重视对碑拓的研究，而且也热衷于对夏、商、周时期青铜器上的铭文和秦汉砖瓦的拓片的研究，出现了大量的拓本及研究专著。可以这样说，在文人的书房里，除了文房用具，最重要的就是碑帖了。

古琴

古琴又称"瑶琴""玉琴""七弦琴"，是世界上最古老的弦乐器之一，也是中国最古老的弹拨乐器。

- 古琴
  Ancient Seven-stringed Zither (*Gu Qin*)

the Zhou Dynasty (1046 B.C.-221 B.C.), and the rubbings of the ancient eaves tiles of the Qin Dynasty and the Han Dynasty were emphasized too. There were abundant inscription copybooks and monographs published. So to speak, in the study of a scholar, aside from the study appliances, the most important object is the inscription copybook.

Ancient Seven-stringed Zither (*Guqin*)

Being one of the oldest string music in the world and performed by China's oldest plucked string instrument: Ancient Seven-stringed Zither (*Guqin*), that also known as the *Yaoqin* or *Yuqin* whose popularity can be dated back to the Spring and Autumn Period (770 B.C.-476 B.C.), *Guqin* music, on which the soul and essence of Chinese music laid, was regarded as the music of Saint. So *Guqin* was also treated as the instrument of Saint, too. With seven strings, the long and narrow body of *Guqin* is often made of fortune paulownia wood or cedar wood and lacquered red. The tone of *Guqin* sounds melodious and penetrating. In Chinese culture, *Guqin* has forged an indissoluble bond with scholar's cultural

• 越窑魂瓶（三国）
Soul Jar, from Yue Kiln (Three Kingdoms Period, 220-280)

• 青釉莲花尊（北魏）
Lotus-shaped Green Glazed Vase (Northern Wei Dynasty, 386-534)

古琴早在春秋时期就已盛行，常被视为圣人之乐、圣人之器，是最能体现中国音乐的灵魂和精髓的乐器之一。古琴狭长的琴身多以桐木或杉木制成，上髹厚漆，有七根弦，音色婉转，穿透力强。在中国文化中，古琴与文人的生活结下了不解之缘。在琴、棋、书、画这四项文人修身之道中，古琴以其静雅的音乐品格，以及所蕴含的文人淡泊名利、超然物外的处世哲学而居于首位。

明器

明器又称"冥器"，是专门为随葬而制作的器物。这些器物有的

life. Because of the quality of clarity and quiet elegance, and the philosophy of life that served as a guide for scholars to be indifferent to fame and wealth and hold themselves aloof from the world, *Guqin* headed the list of four subjects scholars trained themselves in along with chess, calligraphy and painting.

Funerary Ware

A funerary ware, also called burial ware, is a specially produced type of ware buried with the deceased. Among those funerary wares, some were owned by the deceased when they were alive, and others were made out of pottery, porcelain, wood, stone or paper. In addition to copies of daily

是死者生前使用过的，也有的是用陶、瓷、木、石或纸制作的。除了日用器物的仿制品外，还有人物俑、动物俑，以及车、船、建筑物、工具、兵器、家具的模型等。作为书房内被收藏、鉴赏的古玩的明器，主要以汉代和唐代以前的陶俑为主。汉代的明器多为建筑物、动物俑，以及车、船等陶器，有灰釉、褐釉、绿釉等表现形式，造型逼真。秦代流行武士俑，如秦始皇陵的兵马俑大小如真人、真马。魏晋南北朝时期，北方流行武士俑、伎乐俑等，南方则开始流行青瓷明器。唐代的明器多为三彩釉，除了武士俑，还有仕女俑、马俑、骆驼俑等。

necessities, human and animal figurines, model carriages, boats, houses, tools, weapons and building furniture are also seen among funerary wares. The ones appreciated as antique collections and placed in studies are mostly pottery figurines produced between the Han Dynasty and the Tang Dynasty. In the Han Dynasty, most of the funerary wares were pottery animal figurines, model houses and carriages coated with ash, brown and green glaze, vividly molded and true to life, while the Qin Dynasty was the period when warrior figurines were prevailing, led by the unearthed life-size Terra Cotta warriors and horses from Qin the Shihuang's (the first emperor) mausoleum. In the wei, Jin, Southern and Northern dynasties (220-589), warrior figurines, figurines of musicians and dancers were prevalent in North China, while celadon funerary wares in Southern China. The funerary wares produced in the Tang Dynasty were mainly three-color glazed. Besides warrior figurines, lady figurines as well as horse and camel figurines were also produced in the Tang Dynasty.

● 唐三彩马俑（唐）
Three-color Glazed Clay Horse
(Tang Dynasty, 618-907)